# CONTRACT AS

CHARLES FRIED

# CONTRACT AS PROMISE

*A Theory of Contractual Obligation*

Harvard University Press

Cambridge, Massachusetts
and London, England

This book has been digitally reprinted. The content
remains identical to that of previous printings.

Library of Congress Cataloging in Publication Data

Fried, Charles, 1935–
    Contract as promise.
    Includes index.
    1. Contracts.  2. Promise (Law)
I. Title.
K840.F74    346'.02    80-26548

ISBN 0-674-16925-5 (cloth)
ISBN 0-674-16930-1 (paper)

*For Albert M. Sacks*

# PREFACE

This book has two purposes: a theoretical purpose, to show how a complex legal institution, contract, can be traced to and is determined by a small number of basic moral principles; and a pedagogic purpose, to display for students the underlying structure of this basic legal institution. Perhaps there is more legal detail than the theorist requires (as in the discussions of offer and acceptance and conditions) and more theory than is necessary to the law student (as in the early discussion of the morality of promising). Nevertheless I hope that overall the two purposes support each other. At the level of theory I hope to show that the law of contract does have an underlying, unifying structure, and at the level of doctrinal exposition I hope to show that that structure can be referred to moral principles.

## PREFACE

The work grows directly out of the experience of teaching the first-year course in contracts at the Harvard Law School, and my greatest debt is to the students who helped me in and suffered through my attempts to make sense of this complicated subject. My next debt is to the late Lon Fuller, who was my friend and teacher when I was a junior faculty member. I did not then teach contracts and so we rarely discussed that subject in those years, but what I learned from him has combined with my later study of his contract writings and the use of his casebook to leave a powerful impression. I have also profited greatly from numerous conversations with that wisest of contract scholars, John Dawson, from his comments on my draft, and from his writings.

I owe a debt of a different kind, but no less profound, to those scholars and colleagues with whom I am in disagreement. Without the goad of their ingenious and relentless attack on premises I took for granted, I doubt I would have thought it necessary to write this book and I am sure I would not have seen as clearly what the central issues are. I count among those who thus provoked me Patrick Atiyah, Grant Gilmore, Morton Horwitz, and Anthony Kronman, but most particularly my colleagues Duncan Kennedy and Roberto Unger. Unger was particularly kind in sharing with me his unpublished manuscript on contracts and his research notes.

Many friends and colleagues have generously read and commented on earlier drafts: William Andrews, Phillip Areeda, Lucian Bebchuk, Robert Clark, Ronald Dworkin, Richard Epstein, Morton Horwitz, Anthony Kronman, Frank Michelman, Robert Nozick, Todd Rakoff, David Shapiro, Steven Shavell, Judith Thomson, and Arthur von Mehren. Earlier versions of this book were presented in 1978 to faculty workshops at Chicago, Harvard, and Yale Law Schools and to the Society for Ethical and Legal Philosophy. I profited greatly from comments I received on those occasions. Portions were also presented at the University of Indiana Law School as the Harris Lectures and at Osgoode Hall Law School of York University, Toronto, as the 'Or 'Emet Lecture.

I received invaluable research and editorial assistance from several students at the Harvard Law School: Jane Ginsburg and Jane von Frank of the class of 1980; William Ewald of the class of 1981; Donald Board, Gerald Stoddart, and Larry Varn of the class of 1982; and J. Walter Freiberg of the class of 1983.

# CONTENTS

# CONTRACT AS PROMISE

# INTRODUCTION
# THE
# LIFE OF
# CONTRACT

The promise principle, which in this book I argue is the moral basis of contract law, is that principle by which persons may impose on themselves obligations where none existed before.

Security of the person, stability of property, and the obligation of contract were for David Hume the bases of a civilized society.[1] Hume expressed the liberal, individualistic temper of his time and place in treating respect for person, property, and contract as the self-evident foundations of law and justice. Through the greater part of our history, our constitutional law and politics have proceeded on these same premises. In private law particularly these premises have taken root and ramified in the countless particulars necessary to give them substance. The law of property defines the boundaries of our rightful possessions, while the law of torts seeks to make us whole against violations of those boundaries, as well as against violations of the natural boundaries of our physical person.[2] Contract law ratifies and enforces our joint ventures beyond those boundaries. Thus the law of torts and the law of property recognize our rights as individuals in our persons, in our labor, and in some definite portion of the external world, while the law of contracts facilitates our disposing of these rights on terms that seem best to us. The regime of contract law, which respects the dispositions individuals make of their rights, carries to its natural conclusion the liberal premise that individuals have rights.[3] And the will theory of contract, which sees contractual obligations as essentially self-imposed,[4] is a fair implication of liberal individualism.

This conception of contractual obligation as essentially self-imposed has been under increasing pressure over the last fifty years. One essentially historicist line of attack points out that until the eighteenth century communal controls, whether of families, guilds, local communities, or of the general government, hardly conceded enough discretion to individuals over their labor or property to give the liberal conception much to work on. And beginning in the last century and proceeding apace since, the state, unions, corporations, and other intermediate institutions have again withdrawn large areas of concern from individual control and thus from the scope of purely contractual arrangements.[5] That there has been such an ebb and flow of collective control seems fairly clear. But from the fact that contract emerged only in modern times as a principal form of social organization, it does not follow that therefore the concept of contract as promise (which is indeed a centerpiece of nineteenth-century economic liberalism) was itself the invention of the industrial revolution; whatever the accepted scope for contract, the principle of fidelity to one's word is an ancient one.[6] Still less does it follow that the validity, the rightness of the promise principle, of self-imposed obligation, depended on its acceptance in that earlier period, or that now, as the acceptance is in doubt, the validity of the principle is under a cloud. The validity of a moral, like that of a mathematical truth, does not depend on fashion or favor.

A more insidious set of criticisms denies the coherence or the independent viability of the promise principle. Legal obligation can be imposed only by the community, and so in imposing it the community must be pursuing its goals and imposing its standards, rather than neutrally endorsing those of the contracting parties. These lines of attack—found recently in the writings of legal scholars such as Patrick Atiyah, Lawrence Friedman, Grant Gilmore, Morton Horwitz, Duncan Kennedy, Anthony Kronman, and Ian Macneil,[7] as well as in philosophical writings—will provide the foil for much of my affirmative argument. Here I shall just set out their main thrust so that my readers may be clear what I am reacting against.

Not all promises are legally enforced, and of those which are, different categories receive differing degrees of legal recognition: some only if in writing, others between certain kinds of parties, still others only to the extent that they have been relied on and that reliance has caused measurable injury. And some arrangements that are not promissory at all—preliminary negotiations, words mistakenly understood as promises, schemes of cooperation—are assimilated to the contractual regime. Finally, even among legally binding arrangements that are initiated by agreement, certain ones are singled out and made subject to a set of rules that often have little to do with that agreement. Marriage is the most obvious example, but contracts of employment, insurance, or carriage exhibit these features as well. Thus the conception of the will binding itself—the conception at the heart of the promise principle—is neither necessary nor sufficient to contractual obligation. Indeed it is a point of some of these critics (for example, Friedman, Gilmore, Macneil) that the search for a central or unifying principle of contract is a will-o'-the-wisp, an illusion typical of the ill-defined but much excoriated vice of conceptualism.* These critics hold that the law fashions contractual obligation as a way to do justice between, and impose social policy through, parties who have come into a variety of relations with each other. Only some of these relations start in an explicit agreement, and even if they do, the governing considerations of justice and policy are not bound by the terms or implications of that agreement.

Though the bases of contract law on this view are as many and shifting as the politics of the judicial and legislative process, two quite general considerations of justice have figured prominently in the attack on the conception of contract as promise: benefit and reliance. The benefit principle holds that where a person has received a benefit at another's expense and that other has acted reasonably and with no intention of making a gift, fairness requires

---

*On formalism and conceptualism, see chapter 6 infra, at 87-88, and chapter 7 infra, at 102-103.

that the benefit be returned or paid for. I discuss this idea in detail in subsequent chapters. Here I shall make my point by the more pervasive notion of reliance. Proceeding from a theme established in Lon Fuller and William Perdue's influential 1936 article,[8] a number of writers have argued that often what is taken as enforcement of a promise is in reality the compensation of an injury sustained by the plaintiff because he relied on the defendant's promise. At first glance the distinction between promissory obligation and obligation based on reliance may seem too thin to notice, but indeed large theoretical and practical matters turn on that distinction. To enforce a promise as such is to make a defendant render a performance (or its money equivalent) just because he has promised that very thing. The reliance view, by contrast, focuses on an injury suffered by the plaintiff and asks if the defendant is somehow sufficiently responsible for that injury that he should be made to pay compensation.

The latter basis of liability, the compensation of injury suffered through reliance, is a special case of tort liability. For the law of torts is concerned with just the question of compensation for harm caused by another: physical harm caused by willful or negligent conduct, pecuniary harm caused by careless or deceitful representations, injury to reputation caused by untrue statements. Now tort law typically deals with involuntary transactions—if a punch in the nose, a traffic accident, or a malicious piece of gossip may be called a transaction—so that the role of the community in adjudicating the conflict is particularly prominent: What is a safe speed on a rainy evening, what may a former employer say in response to a request for a reference? In contrast, so long as we see contractual obligation as based on promise, on obligations that the parties have themselves assumed, the focus of the inquiry is on the will of the parties. If we assimilate contractual obligation to the law of torts,[9] our focus shifts to the injury suffered by the plaintiff and to the fairness of saddling the defendant with some or all of it. So, for instance, if there has been no palpable injury because the promisee has not yet relied on the promise there seems to be nothing to compensate, while at other times a generalized standard of fair compensation may move us to go beyond anything that the parties have agreed. The promise and its sequellae are seen as a kind of encounter, like a traffic accident or a street altercation or a journalistic exchange, giving rise to losses to be apportioned by the community's sense of fairness. This assimilation of contract to tort is (and for writers like Gilmore, Horwitz, and

4

Atiyah is intended to be) the subordination of a quintessentially individualist ground for obligation and form of social control, one that refers to the will of the parties, to a set of standards that are ineluctably collective in origin and thus readily turned to collective ends.*

Another line of attack on contract as promise denies the coherence of the central idea of self-imposed obligation. Some writers argue that obligation must always be imposed from outside.[10] Others work from within: For promissory obligations to be truly self-imposed, the promise must have been freely given. If this means no more than that the promisor acted intentionally, then even an undertaking in response to a gunman's threat is binding. If, as we must, we insist that there be a *fair* choice to promise or not, we have imported external standards of fairness into the very heart of the obligation after all. Having said, for instance, that a promise to pay an exorbitant price for a vital medicine is not freely undertaken, while a promise to pay a reasonable price is, why not dispense with the element of promise altogether and just hold that there is an obligation to supply the medicine at an externally fixed price to all who need it? This and more subtle related suggestions have been put forward by writers who are particularly concerned about the connection between contract as promise and the market as a form of economic organization. Some like Robert Hale, Duncan Kennedy, and Anthony Kronman[11] see in the concepts of duress and unconscionability the undoing of the arguments for the free market and for the autonomy of contract law. Others, most particularly Richard Posner,[12] also denying any independent force to promissory obligation, derive such force as the law gives to contracts from social policies such as wealth maximization and efficiency, which are usually associated with the operation of the market.

I begin with a statement of the central conception of contract as

---

*The two ideas—obligation based on promise and obligation based on fair compensation of injury suffered through reliance—can be run together. One may say that a disappointed expectation is a compensable injury without more, and that the giving of a promise is a sufficient (perhaps even a necessary) ground for holding a promisor responsible for such an injury. This is obviously not what the "Death of Contract" theorists have in mind. For them a cognizable injury must be a palpable loss identifiable apart from the expectation that the promise will be kept: for instance some expense that would not otherwise have been undertaken and that cannot be recouped, or some precaution omitted with ensuing loss. The distinction becomes rather thin when we consider opportunity costs—profitable bargains we might have made had we not relied on this one being kept—especially since those alternative bargains might themselves have been cast in promissory form (but those promises in turn might or might not have been honored).

promise. This is my version of the classical view of contract proposed by the will theory and implicit in the assertion that contract offers a distinct and compelling ground of obligation. In subsequent chapters I show how this conception generates the structure and accounts for the complexities of contract doctrine. Contract law is complex, and it is easy to lose sight of its essential unity. The adherents of the "Death of Contract" school have been left too free a rein to exploit these complexities. But exponents of the view I embrace have often adopted a far more rigid approach than the theory of contract as promise requires. For instance, they have typically tended to view contractual liability as an exclusive principle of fairness, as if relief had to be either based on a promise or denied altogether. These rigidities and excesses have also been exploited as if they proved the whole conception of contract as promise false. In developing my affirmative thesis I show why classical theory may have betrayed itself into such errors, and I propose to perennial conundrums solutions that accord with the idea of contract as promise and with decency and common sense as well.

## 2

# CONTRACT
# AS
# PROMISE

Ⅰt is a first principle of liberal political morality that we be secure in what is ours — so that our persons and property not be open to exploitation by others, and that from a sure foundation we may express our will and expend our powers in the world. By these powers we may create good things or low, useful articles or luxuries, things extraordinary or banal, and we will be judged accordingly — as saintly or mean, skillful or ordinary, industrious and fortunate or debased, friendly and kind or cold and inhuman. But whatever we accomplish and however that accomplishment is judged, morality requires that we respect the person and property of others, leaving them free to make their lives as we are left free to make ours. This is the liberal ideal. This is the ideal that distinguishes between the good, which is the domain of aspiration, and the right, which sets the terms and limits according to which we strive. This ideal makes what we achieve our own and our failures our responsibility too—however much or little we may choose to share our good fortune and however we may hope for help when we fail.[1]

Everything must be available to us, for who can deny the human will the title to expand even into the remotest corner of the universe? And when we forbear to bend some external object to our use because of its natural preciousness we use it still, for it is to our judgment of its value that we respond, our own conception of the good that we pursue. Only other persons are not available to us in this way—they alone share our self-consciousness, our power of self-determination; thus to use them as if they were merely part of external nature is to poison the source of the moral power we enjoy. But others *are* part of the external world, and by denying ourselves access to their persons and powers, we drastically shrink the scope of our efficacy. So it was a crucial moral discovery that free men may yet freely serve each others' purposes: the discovery that beyond the fear of reprisal or the hope of reciprocal favor, morality itself might be enlisted to assure not only that you respect me and mine but that you actively serve my purposes.[2] When my confidence in your assistance derives from my conviction that you will do what is right (not just what is prudent), then I trust you, and trust becomes a powerful tool for our working our mutual wills in the world. So remarkable a tool is trust that in the end we pursue it for its own sake; we prefer doing things cooperatively when we might have relied on fear or interest or worked alone.[3]

The device that gives trust its sharpest, most palpable form is promise. By promising we put in another man's hands a new power to accomplish his will, though only a moral power: What he sought to do alone he may now expect to do with our promised help, and to give him this new facility was our very purpose in promising. By promising we transform a choice that was morally neutral into one that is morally compelled. Morality, which must be permanent and beyond our particular will if the grounds for our willing are to be secure, is itself invoked, molded to allow us better to work that particular will. Morality then serves modest, humdrum ends: We make appointments, buy and sell, harnessing this loftiest of all forces.

What is a promise, that by my words I should make wrong what before was morally indifferent? A promise is a communication — usually verbal; it says something. But how can my saying something put a moral charge on a choice that before was morally neutral? Well, by my misleading you, or by lying.[4] Is lying not the very paradigm of doing wrong by speaking? But this won't do, for a promise puts the moral charge on a *potential* act — the wrong is done later, when the promise is not kept — while a lie is a wrong committed at the time of its utterance. Both wrongs abuse trust, but in different ways. When I speak I commit myself to the truth of my utterance, but when I promise I commit myself to *act*, later. Though these two wrongs are thus quite distinct there has been a persistent tendency to run them together by treating a promise as a lie after all, but a particular kind of lie: a lie about one's intentions. Consider this case:

I. I sell you a house, retaining an adjacent vacant lot. At the time of our negotiations, I state that I intend to build a home for myself on that lot. What if several years later I sell the lot to a person who builds a gas station on it? What if I sell it only one month later? What if I am already negotiating for its sale as a gas station at the time I sell the house to you?[5]

If I was already negotiating to sell the lot for a gas station at the time of my statement to you, I have wronged you. I have lied to you about the state of my intentions, and this is as much a lie as a lie about the state of the plumbing.[6] If, however, I sell the lot many years later, I do you no wrong. There are no grounds for saying I lied about my intentions; I have just changed my mind. Now if I had *promised* to use the lot only as a residence, the situation would be different. Promising is more than just truthfully reporting my present intentions, for I may be free to change my mind, as I am not free to break my promise.

Let us take it as given here that lying is wrong and so that it is wrong to obtain benefits or cause harm by lying (including lying about one's intentions). It does not at all follow that to obtain a benefit or cause harm by breaking a promise is also wrong. That my act procures me a benefit or causes harm all by itself proves nothing. If I open a restaurant near your hotel and prosper as I draw your guests away from the standard hotel fare you offer, this benefit I draw from you places me under no obligation to you. I should make restitution only if I benefit *unjustly,* which I do if I deceive you—as when I lie to you about my intentions in example I.[7] But where is the injustice if I honestly intend to keep my promise at the time of making it, and later change my mind? If we feel I owe you recompense in that case too, it cannot be because of the benefit I have obtained through my promise: We have seen that benefit even at another's expense is not alone sufficient to require compensation. If I owe you a duty to return that benefit it must be because of the promise. It is the promise that makes my enrichment at your expense unjust, and not the enrichment that makes the promise binding. And thus neither the statement of intention nor the benefit explains why, if at all, a promise does any moral work.

A more common attempt to reduce the force of a promise to some other moral category invokes the harm you suffer in relying on my promise. My statement is like a pit I have dug in the road, into which you fall. I have harmed you and should make you whole. Thus the tort principle might be urged to bridge the gap in the argument between a statement of intention and a promise: I have a duty just because I could have foreseen (indeed it was my intention) that you would rely on my promise and that you would suffer harm when I broke it. And this wrong then not only sets the stage for compensation of the harm caused by the misplaced reliance, but also supplies the moral predicate for restitution of any benefits I may have extracted from you on the strength of my promise.[8] But we still beg the question. If the promise is no more than a truthful statement of my intention, why am *I* responsible for harm that befalls you as a result of my change of heart? To be sure, it is not like a change in the weather—I might have kept to my original intention—but how does this distinguish the broken promise from any other statement of intention (or habit or prediction of future conduct) of mine of which you know and on which you choose to rely? Should your expectations of me limit my freedom of choice? If you rent the apartment next to mine because I play chamber music there, do I owe you more than an expression of regret when my friends and I decide to meet instead at the cellist's home? And in general, why should my liberty be constrained by the harm you would suffer from the disappointment of the expectations you choose to entertain about my choices?

Does it make a difference that when I promise you do not just happen to rely on me, that I communicate my intention to you and therefore can be taken to know that changing my mind may put you at risk? But then I might be aware that you would count on my keeping to my intentions even if I myself had not communicated those intentions to you. (*You* might have told me you were relying on me, or you might have overheard me telling some third person of my intentions.) It might be said that I become the agent of your reliance by telling you, and that this makes my responsibility clearer: After all, I can scarcely control all the ways in which you might learn of my intentions, but I *can* control whether or not I tell you of them. But we are still begging the question. If promising is no more than my telling you of my intentions, why do we both not know that I may yet change my mind? Perhaps, then, promising is like telling you of my intention and telling you that I don't intend to change my mind. But why can't I change my mind about the latter intention?

Perhaps the statement of intention in promising is binding because we not only foresee reliance, we invite it: We intend the promisee to rely on the promise. Yet even this will not do. If I invite reliance on my stated intention, then that is all I invite. Certainly I may hope and intend, in example I, that you buy my house on the basis of what I have told you, but why does that hope bind me to do more than state my intention honestly? And that intention and invitation are quite compatible with my later changing my mind. In every case, of course, I should weigh the harm I will do if I do change my mind. If I am a doctor and I know you will rely on me to be part of an outing on which someone may fall ill, I should certainly weigh the harm that may come about if that reliance is disappointed. Indeed I should weigh that harm even if you do not rely on me, but are foolish enough not to have made a provision for a doctor. Yet in none of these instances am I bound as I would be had I promised.[9]

A promise invokes trust in my future actions, not merely in my present sincerity. We need to isolate an additional element, over and above benefit, reliance, and the communication of intention. That additional element must *commit* me, and commit me to more than the truth of some statement. That additional element has so far eluded our analysis.

It has eluded us, I believe, because there is a real puzzle about how we can commit ourselves to a course of conduct that absent our commitment is morally neutral. The invocation of benefit and reliance are attempts to explain the force of a promise in terms of two of its most usual effects, but the attempts fail because these effects depend on the prior assumption of the force of the commitment. The way out of the puzzle is to recognize the bootstrap quality of the argument: To have force in *a particular case* promises must be assumed to have force generally. Once that general assumption is made, the effects we intentionally produce by a particular promise may be morally attributed to us. This recognition is not as paradoxical as its abstract statement here may make it seem. It lies, after all, behind every conventional structure: games,[10] institutions and practices, and most important, language.

Let us put to one side the question of how a convention comes into being, or of when and why we are morally bound to comply with its terms, while we look briefly at what a convention is and how it does its work. Take the classical example of a game. What the players do is defined by a system of rules—sometimes quite vague and informal, sometimes elaborate and codified. These rules apply only to the players—that is, to persons who invoke them. These rules are a human invention, and their consequences (castling, striking out, winning, losing) can be understood only in terms of the rules. The players may have a variety of motives for playing (profit, fun, maybe even duty to fellow players who need participants). A variety of judgments are applicable to the players—they may be deemed skillful, imaginative, bold, honest, or dishonest—but these judgments and motives too can be understood only in the context of the game. For instance, you can cheat only by breaking rules to which you pretend to conform.

This almost canonical invocation of the game example has often been misunderstood as somehow applying only to unserious matters, to play, so that it is said to trivialize the solemn objects (like law or promises) that it is used to explain. But this is a mistake, confusing the interests involved, the reasons for creating and invoking a particular convention, with the logical structure of conventions in general. Games are (often) played for fun, but other conventions—for instance religious rituals or legal procedures—may have most earnest ends, while still other conventions are quite general. To the last category belongs language. The conventional nature of language is too obvious to belabor. It is worth pointing out, however, that the various things we do with language—informing, reporting, promising, insulting, cheating, lying—all depend on the conventional structure's being firmly in place. You could not lie if there were not both understanding of the language you lied in and a general convention of using that language truthfully. This point holds irrespective of whether the institution of language has advanced the situation of mankind and of whether lying is sometimes, always, or never wrong.

Promising too is a very general convention — though less general than language, of course, since promising is itself a use of language.[11] The convention of promising (like that of language) has a very general purpose under which we may bring an infinite set of particular purposes. In order that I be as free as possible, that my will have the greatest possible range consistent with the similar will of others, it is necessary that there be a way in which I may commit myself. It is necessary that I be able to make nonoptional a course of conduct that would otherwise be optional for me. By doing this I can facilitate the projects of others, because I can make it possible for those others to count on my future conduct, and thus those others can pursue more intricate, more far-reaching projects. If it is my purpose, my will that others be able to count on me in the pursuit of their endeavor, it is essential that I be able to deliver myself into their hands more firmly than where they simply predict my future course. Thus the possibility of commitment permits an act of generosity on my part, permits me to pursue a project whose content is that *you* be permitted to pursue *your* project. But of course this purely altruistic motive is not the only motive worth facilitating. More central to our concern is the situation where we facilitate each other's projects, where the gain is reciprocal. Schematically the situation looks like this:

You want to accomplish purpose A and I want to accomplish purpose B. Neither of us can succeed without the cooperation of the other. Thus I want to be able to commit myself to help you achieve A so that you will commit yourself to help me achieve B.

Now if A and B are objects or actions that can be transferred simultaneously there is no need for commitment. As I hand over A you hand over B, and we are both satisfied. But very few things are like that. We need a device to permit a trade over time: to allow me to do A for you when you need it, in the confident belief that you will do B for me when I need it. Your commitment puts your future performance into my hands in the present just as my commitment puts my future performance into your hands. A future exchange is transformed into a present exchange. And in order to accomplish this all we need is a conventional device which we both invoke, which you know I am invoking when I invoke it, which I know that you know I am invoking, and so on.

The only mystery about this is the mystery that surrounds increasing autonomy by providing means for restricting it. But really this is a pseudomystery. The restrictions involved in promising are restrictions undertaken just in order to increase one's options in the long run, and thus are perfectly consistent with the principle of autonomy—consistent with a respect for one's own autonomy and the autonomy of others. To be sure, in getting something for myself now by promising to do something for you in the future, I am mortgaging the interest of my future self in favor of my present self. How can I be sure my future self will approve?* This is a deep and difficult problem about which I say more later in this chapter. Suffice it to say here that unless one assumes the continuity of the self and the possibility of maintaining complex projects over time, not only the morality of promising but also any coherent picture of the person becomes impossible.

## THE MORAL OBLIGATION OF PROMISE

Once I have invoked the institution of promising, why exactly is it wrong for me then to break my promise?

My argument so far does not answer that question. The institution of promising is a way for me to bind myself to another so that the other may expect a future performance, and binding myself in this way is something that I may want to be able to do. But this by itself does not show that I am morally obligated to perform my promise at a later time if to do so proves inconvenient or costly. That there should be a system of currency also increases my options and is useful to me, but this does not show why I should not use counterfeit money if I can get away with it. In just the same way the usefulness of promising in general does not show why I should not take advantage of it in a particular case and yet fail to keep my promise. That the convention would cease to function in the long run, would cease

*Note that this problem does not arise where I make a present sacrifice for a future benefit, since by hypothesis I am presently willing to make that sacrifice and in the future I only stand to gain.

to provide benefits if everyone felt free to violate it, is hardly an answer to the question of why I should keep a particular promise on a particular occasion.

David Lewis has shown[12] that a convention that it would be in each person's interest to observe if everyone else observed it will be established and maintained without any special mechanisms of commitment or enforcement. Starting with simple conventions (for example that if a telephone conversation is disconnected, the person who initiated the call is the one who calls back) Lewis extends his argument to the case of language. Now promising is different, since (unlike language, where it is overwhelmingly in the interest of all that everyone comply with linguistic conventions, even when language is used to deceive) it will often be in the interest of the promisor *not* to conform to the convention when it comes time to render his performance. Therefore individual self-interest is not enough to sustain the convention, and some additional ground is needed to keep it from unraveling. There are two principal candidates: external sanctions and moral obligation.

David Hume sought to combine these two by proposing that the external sanction of public opprobrium, of loss of reputation for honesty, which society attaches to promise-breaking, is internalized, becomes instinctual, and accounts for the sense of the moral obligation of promise.[13] Though Hume offers a possible anthropological or psychological account of how people feel about promises, his is not a satisfactory *moral* argument. Assume that I can get away with breaking my promise (the promisee is dead), and I am now asking why I should keep it anyway in the face of some personal inconvenience. Hume's account of obligation is more like an argument *against* my keeping the promise, for it tells me how any feelings of obligation that I may harbor have come to lodge in my psyche and thus is the first step toward ridding me of such inconvenient prejudices.

Considerations of self-interest cannot supply the moral basis of my obligation to keep a promise. By an analogous argument neither can considerations of utility. For however sincerely and impartially I may apply the utilitarian injunction to consider at each step how I might increase the sum of happiness or utility in the world, it will allow me to break my promise whenever the balance of advantage (including, of course, my own advantage) tips in that direction. The possible damage to the institution of promising is only one factor in the calculation. Other factors are the alternative good I might do by breaking my promise, whether and by how many people the breach might be discovered, what the actual effect on confidence of such a breach would be. There is no a priori reason for believing that an individual's calculations will come out in favor of keeping the promise always, sometimes, or most of the time.

Rule-utilitarianism seeks to offer a way out of this conundrum. The individual's moral obligation is determined not by what the best action at a particular moment would be, but by the rule it would be best for him to follow. It has, I believe, been demonstrated that this position is incoherent: Either rule-utilitarianism requires that rules be followed in a particular case even where the result would not be best all things considered, and so the utilitarian aspect of rule-utilitarianism is abandoned; or the obligation to follow the rule is so qualified as to collapse into act-utilitarianism after all.[14] There is, however, a version of rule-utilitarianism that makes a great deal of sense. In this version the utilitarian does not instruct us what our individual moral obligations are but rather instructs legislators what the best rules are.[15] If legislation is our focus, then the contradictions of rule-utilitarianism do not arise, since we are instructing those whose decisions can *only* take the form of issuing rules. From that perspective there is obvious utility to rules establishing and enforcing promissory obligations. Since I am concerned now with the question of individual obligation, that is, morai obligation, this legislative perspective on the argument is not available to me.

The obligation to keep a promise is grounded not in arguments of utility but in respect for individual autonomy and in trust. Autonomy and trust are grounds for the institution of promising as well, but the argument for *individual* obligation is not the same. Individual obligation is only a step away, but that step must be taken.[16] An individual is morally bound to keep his promises because he has intentionally invoked a convention whose function it is to give grounds—moral grounds—for another to expect the promised performance.[17] To renege is to abuse a confidence he was free to invite or not, and which he intentionally did invite. To abuse that confidence now is like (but only *like*) lying: the abuse of a shared social institution that is intended to invoke the bonds of trust. A liar and a promise-breaker each *use* another person. In both speech and promising there is an invitation to the other to trust, to make himself vulnerable; the liar and the promise-breaker then abuse that trust.

The obligation to keep a promise is thus similar to but more constraining than the obligation to tell the truth. To avoid lying you need only believe in the truth of what you say when you say it, but a promise binds into the future, well past the moment when the promise is made. There will, of course, be great social utility to a general regime of trust and confidence in promises and truthfulness. But this just shows that a regime of mutual respect allows men and women to accomplish what in a jungle of unrestrained self-interest could not be accomplished. If this advantage is to be firmly established, there must exist a ground for mutual confidence deeper than and independent of the social utility it permits.

The utilitarian counting the advantages affirms the general importance of enforcing *contracts*. The moralist of duty, however, sees *promising* as a device that free, moral individuals have fashioned on the premise of mutual trust, and which gathers its moral force from that premise. The moralist of duty thus posits a general obligation to keep promises, of which the obligation of contract will be only a special case—that special case in which certain promises have attained legal as well as moral force. But since a contract is first of all a promise, the contract must be kept because a promise must be kept.

To summarize: There exists a convention that defines the practice of promising and its entailments. This convention provides a way that a person may create expectations in others. By virtue of the basic Kantian principles of trust and respect, it is wrong to invoke that convention in order to make a promise, and then to break it.

## WHAT A PROMISE IS WORTH

If I make a promise to you, I should do as I promise; and if I fail to keep my promise, it is fair that I should be made to hand over the equivalent of the promised performance. In contract doctrine this proposition appears as the expectation measure of damages for breach. The expectation standard gives the victim of a breach no more or less than he would have had had there been no breach—in other words, he gets the benefit of his bargain.[18] Two alternative measures of damage, reliance and restitution, express the different notions that if a person has relied on a promise and been hurt, that hurt must be made good; and that if a contract-breaker has obtained goods or services, he must be made to pay a fair (just?) price for them.[19] Consider three cases:

17

II-A. I enter your antique shop on a quiet afternoon and agree in writing to buy an expensive chest I see there, the price being about three times what you paid for it a short time ago. When I get home I repent of my decision, and within half an hour of my visit—before any other customer has come to your store—I telephone to say I no longer want the chest.

II-B. Same as above, except in the meantime you have waxed and polished the chest and had your delivery van bring it to my door.

II-C. Same as above, except I have the use of the chest for six months, while your shop is closed for renovations.

To require me to pay for the chest in case II-A (or, if you resell it, to pay any profit you lost, including lost business volume) is to give you your expectation, the benefit of your bargain. In II-B if all I must compensate is your effort I am reimbursing your reliance, and in II-C to force me to pay a fair price for the use I have had of the chest is to focus on making me pay for, restore, an actual benefit I have received.

The assault on the classical conception of contract, the concept I call contract as promise, has centered on the connection—taken as canonical for some hundred years—between contract law and expectation damages. To focus the attack on this connection is indeed strategic. As the critics recognize and as I have just stated, to the extent that contract is grounded in promise, it seems natural to measure relief by the expectation, that is, by the promise itself. If that link can be threatened, then contract itself may be grounded elsewhere than in promise, elsewhere than in the will of the parties. In his recent comprehensive treatise, *The Rise and Fall of Freedom of Contract*, Patrick Atiyah makes the connection between the recourse to expectation damages and the emerging enforceability of executory contracts—that is, contracts enforced, though no detriment has been suffered in reliance and no benefit has been conferred. (Case II-A is an example of an executory contract.) Before the nineteenth century, he argues, a contractual relation referred generally to one of a number of particular, community-sanctioned relations between persons who in the course of their dealings (as carriers, innkeepers, surgeons, merchants) relied on each other to their detriment or conferred benefits on each other. It was these detriments and benefits that had to be reimbursed, and an explicit promise—if there happened to be one—was important primarily to establish the reliance or to show that the benefit had been conferred in expectation of payment, not officiously or as a gift. All this, Atiyah writes, turned inside out when the promise itself came to be seen as the basis of obligation, so that neither benefit nor reliance any longer seemed necessary and the proper measure of the obligation was the promise itself, that is, the expectation. The promise principle was embraced as an expression of the principle of liberty— the will binding itself, to use Kantian language, rather than being bound by the norms of the collectivity—and the award of expectation damages followed as a natural concomitant of the promise principle.

The insistence on reliance or benefit is related to disputes about the nature of promising. As I have argued, reliance on a promise cannot alone explain its force: There is reliance because a promise is binding, and not the other way around. But if a person is bound by his promise and not by the harm the promisee may have suffered in reliance on it, then what he is bound to is just its performance. Put simply, I am bound to do what I promised you I would do—or I am bound to put you in as good a position as if I had done so. To bind me to do no more than to reimburse your reliance is to excuse me to that extent from the obligation I undertook. If your reliance is less than your expectation (in case II-A there is no reliance), then to that extent a reliance standard excuses me from the very obligation I undertook and so weakens the force of an obligation I chose to assume. Since by hypothesis I chose to assume the obligation in its stronger form (that is, to render the performance promised), the reliance rule indeed precludes me from incurring the very obligation I chose to undertake at the time of promising. The most compelling of the arguments for resisting this conclusion and for urging that we settle for reliance is the sense that it is sometimes harsh and ungenerous to insist on the full measure of expectancy. (This is part of Atiyah's thrust when he designates the expectation standard as an aspect of the rigid Victorian promissory morality.) The harshness comes about because in the event the promisor finds the obligation he assumed too burdensome.

This distress may be analyzed into three forms: (1) The promisor regrets having to pay for what he has bought (which may only have been the satisfaction of promising a gift or the thrill of buying a lottery ticket or stock option), though he would readily do the same thing again. I take it that this kind of regret merits no sympathy at all. Indeed if we gave in to it we would frustrate the promisor's ability to engage in his own continuing projects and so the promisor's plea is, strictly speaking, self-contradictory. (2) The promisor regrets his promise because he was mistaken about the nature of the burdens he was assuming—the purchaser in case II-A thought he would find the money for the antique but in fact his savings are depleted, or perhaps the chest is not as old nor as valuable as he had imagined, or his house has burned down and he no longer needs it. All of these regrets are based on mistaken assumptions about the facts as they are or as they turn out to be. As we shall see in chapter 5, the doctrines of mistake, frustration, and impossibility provide grounds for mitigating the effect of the promise principle without at all undermining it.

Finally there is the most troublesome ground of regret: (3) The promisor made no mistake about the facts or probabilities at all, but now that it has come time to perform he no longer values the promise as highly as when he made it. He regrets the promise because he regrets the value judgment that led him to make it. He concludes that the purchase of an expensive antique is an extravagance. Compassion may lead a promisee to release an obligation in such a case, but he releases as an act of generosity, not as a duty, and certainly not because the promisor's repentance destroys the force of the original obligation. The intuitive reason for holding fast is that such repentance should be the promisor's own responsibility, not one he can shift onto others. It seems too easy a way of getting out of one's obligations. Yet our intuition does not depend on suspicions of insincerity alone. Rather we feel that holding people to their obligations is a way of taking them seriously and thus of giving the concept of sincerity itself serious content. Taking this intuition to a more abstract level, I would say that respect for others as free and rational requires taking seriously their capacity to determine their own values. I invoke again the distinction between the right and the good. The right defines the concept of the self as choosing its own conception of the good. Others must respect our capacity as free and rational persons to choose our own good, and that respect means allowing persons to take responsibility for the good they choose. And, of course, that choosing self is not an instantaneous self but one extended in time, so that to respect those determinations of the self is to respect their persistence over time. If we decline to take seriously the assumption of an obligation because we do not take seriously the promisor's prior conception of the good that led him to assume it, to that extent we do not take him seriously as a person. We infantilize him, as we do quite properly when we release the very young from the consequences of their choices.[20]

Since contracts invoke and are invoked by promises, it is not surprising that the law came to impose on the promises it recognized the same incidents as morality demands. The connection between contract and the expectation principle is so palpable that there is reason to doubt that its legal recognition is a relatively recent invention. It is true that over the last two centuries citizens in the liberal democracies have become increasingly free to dispose of their talents, labor, and property as seems best to them. The freedom to bind oneself contractually to a future disposition is an important and striking example of this freedom (the freedom to make testamentary dispositions or to make whatever present use of one's effort or goods one desires are other examples), because in a promise one is taking responsibility not only for one's present self but for one's future self. But this does not argue that the promise principle itself is a novelty—surely Cicero's, Pufendorf's and Grotius's discussions of it[21] show that it is not—but only that its use has expanded greatly over the years.

## REMEDIES IN AND AROUND THE PROMISE

Those who have an interest in assimilating contract to the more communitarian standards of tort law have been able to obscure the link between contract and promise because in certain cases the natural thing to do *is* to give damages for the harm that has been suffered, rather than to give the money value of the promised expectation. But it does not follow from these cases that expectation is not a normal and natural measure for contract damages. First, these are situations in which the harm suffered is the measure of damages because it is hard to find the monetary value of the expectation. A leading case, *Security Stove & Mfg. Co. v. American Railway Express Co.*,[22] illustrates the type. The plaintiff stove manufacturer had arranged to have a new kind of stove shipped by the defendant express company to a trade convention, at which the plaintiff hoped to interest prospective buyers in his improved product. The president and his workmen went to the convention, but the defendant failed to deliver a crucial part of the exhibit in time, and they had nothing to show. Plaintiff brought suit to recover the cost of renting the booth, the freight charges, and the time and expenses lost as a result of the fruitless trip to the convention. The recovery of these items of damages, which (with the possible exception of the prepaid booth rental) seem typical examples of reliance losses, is generally agreed to have been appropriate. There was no way of knowing what results the plaintiff would have obtained had he succeeded in exhibiting his product at the convention. There was no way of knowing what his expectancy was, and so the court gave him his loss through reliance. But this illustrates only that where expectancy cannot be calculated, reliance may be a reasonable surrogate. It is reasonable to suppose that the plaintiff's expectation in *Security Stove* was at least as great as the monies he put out to exhibit his goods—after all, he was a businessman and is assumed to have been exhibiting his goods to make an eventual profit. If it could somehow be shown that the exhibit would have been a failure and the plaintiff would have suffered a net loss, the case for recovery would be undermined, and most authorities would then deny recovery.*[23]

Second are the cases in which the amount needed to undo the harm caused by reliance is itself the fairest measure of expectation.

> III-A. Buyer approaches manufacturer with the specifications of a small, inexpensive part—say a bolt—for a machine buyer is building. Manufacturer selects the part and sells it to buyer. The bolt is badly made, shears, and damages the machine.

The value of the thing promised, a well-made bolt, is negligible, but to give buyer his money back and no more would be a grave injustice. Here it does seem more natural to say that the manufacturer induced buyer's reasonable reliance and should compensate the resulting harm. But it is equally the case that it is a fair implication of the simple-seeming original transaction that manufacturer not only delivered and promised to transfer good title to the bolt, but promised

---

*A case like this may be seen as involving no more than the allocation of the burden of proof as to the expectation. The plaintiff shows his reliance costs and says that prima facie his expectation was at least that great. The burden then shifts to the defendant to show that indeed this was a losing proposition and the expectation was less than the reliance. It seems only fair that since the defendant's breach prevented the exhibition from taking place and thus prevented the drama on which the expectation depended from being played out, the defendant should at least bear the risk of showing that the venture would have been a failure.

at the same time that the bolt would do the job it was meant to do.*[24]

It is for the (perhaps wholly innocent) breach of this implied promise that we hold manufacturers liable. The soundness of this analysis is brought home if we vary the facts slightly:

III-B. Same as above, except buyer purchases the bolt over the counter in a local hardware store, saying nothing about its use.

To make the owner of the hardware store or the manufacturer of the bolt responsible for large damages in this case seems unfair. One can say that this is because they could not *foresee* harm of this magnitude arising out of their conduct. (A tort locution: The man who negligently jostles a package containing a bomb could not *foresee* and is not responsible for harm of the ensuing magnitude when the package explodes.) But one can as well cast the matter again in contractual terms, saying that they did not undertake this measure of responsibility. After all, if in the first version of this example the buyer and manufacturer had agreed that manufacturer would be responsible only up to a certain amount, say ten times the cost of the bolt, such a limitation would generally be respected. So in certain cases tort and contract ideas converge on the same result.[25] In III-A we may say that buyer justifiably relied on manufacturer. He relied in part because of the (implied) promise or warranty, and of course it *is* a primary function of promises to induce reliance.

Consider finally this variation:

III-C. Manufacturer makes not bolts but tinned goods. Buyer buys a can of peas at a grocer's and serves them to a guest who chips a tooth on a stone negligently included in the can.

Manufacturer promised the guest nothing. (In legal terminology there is between them no privity of contract.) Yet manufacturer should be responsible for the guest's injuries, just as the driver of a car should be responsible for the injuries of a pedestrian whom he negligently hits, though there too privity of contract is lacking.[26]

---

*In law the latter promise is called a warranty—a promise not merely that the promisor will do something in the future, but a taking of responsibility over and above the responsibility of well-meaning honesty that something is the case. For instance, a dealer may warrant that a violin is a Stradivarius. This means more than that he in good faith believes it to be one: he is promising that if it is not, he will be responsible. Uniform Commercial Code (hereafter cited as UCC) § 2-714. Cf. Smith v. Zimbalist, 2 Cal. App.2d 324, 38 P.2d 170 (1934), hearing denied 17 Jan. 1935.

One may say that the guest reasonably relied on the purity of the peas he ate, just as a pedestrian must rely on the due care of motorists. But I never argued that promise is the *only* basis of reliance or that contract is the only basis of responsibility for harms to others.

Third, there are cases in which wrongs are committed and loss is suffered in and around the attempt to make an agreement. In these cases too reliance is the best measure of compensation. A striking example is *Hoffman v. Red Owl Stores:*[27] A prospective Red Owl supermarket franchisee sold his previously owned business and made other expenditures on the assumption that his negotiations to obtain a Red Owl franchise would shortly be concluded. The award of reliance damages was not a case of enforcement of a promise at all, since the parties had not reached the stage where clearly determined promises had been made. Reliance damages were awarded because Red Owl had not dealt fairly with Hoffman. It had allowed him to incur expenses based on hopes that Red Owl knew or should have known were imprudent and that Red Owl was not prepared to permit him to realize. Red Owl was held liable not in order to force it to perform a promise, which it had never made, but rather to compensate Hoffman for losses he had suffered through Red Owl's inconsiderate and temporizing assurances.[28] There is nothing at all in my conception of contract as promise that precludes persons who behave badly and cause unnecessary harm from being forced to make fair compensation. Promissory obligation is not the only basis for liability; principles of tort are sufficient to provide that people who give vague assurances that cause foreseeable harm to others should make compensation. Cases like *Hoffman* are seen to undermine the conception of contract as promise: If contract is really discrete and if it is really based in promise, then whenever there has been a promise in the picture (even only a potential promise) contractual principles must govern the whole relation. To state the argument is to reveal it as a non sequitur. It is a logical fallacy of which the classical exponents of contract as promise were themselves supremely guilty in their reluctance to grant relief for fraud or for mistakes that prevented a real agreement from coming into being. Modern critics of contractual freedom have taken the classics at their word. Justice often requires relief and adjustment in cases of accidents in and around the contracting process, and the critics have seen in this a refutation of the classics' major premise. In chapter 5, which deals with mistake, impossibility and frustration, I will show in detail how the excessive rigidity of the classics played both them and the concept of contract as promise false. Here it is sufficient to introduce the notion that contract as promise has a distinct but neither exclusive nor necessarily dominant place among legal and moral principles. A major concern of this book is the articulation of the boundaries and connection between the promissory and other principles of justice.*

The tendency to merge promise into its adjacent concepts applies also to the relation between it and the principle of restitution, which holds that a person who has received a benefit at another's expense should compensate his benefactor, unless a gift was intended. This principle does indeed appeal to a primitive intuition of fairness. Even where a gift was intended, the appropriateness at least of gratitude if not of a vague duty to reciprocate is recognized in many cultures. Aristotle refers the principle to the imperative that some balance be retained among members of a society, but this seems to restate the proposition rather than to explain it.[29] Since restitution, like reliance, is a principle of fairness that operates independently of the will of the parties, the attempt to refer promissory obligation to this principle is another attempt to explain away the self-imposed character of promissory obligation. I have already argued that this cannot be done without begging the question. Certainly the restitution principle cannot explain the force of a promise for which no benefit has yet been or ever will be given in return. (The legal recognition of such gift promises is tangled in the confusions of the doctrine of consideration, which is the subject of chapter 3.) The reduction of promise to restitution (or to restitution plus reliance) must fail. There are nevertheless breaches of promise for which restitution is the correct principle of relief.[30]

IV. In a case like *Security Stove,* where the freight charges have been prepaid but the goods never picked up or delivered as

---

*There is a category of cases that has become famous in the law under the rubric of promissory estoppel or detrimental reliance. In these cases there has indeed generally been a promise, but the basis for *legal* redress is said to be the plaintiff's detrimental reliance on the promise. Courts now tend to limit the amount of the redress in such cases to the detriment suffered through reliance. But these cases also do not show that reliance and harm are the general basis for contractual recovery. Rather these cases should be seen for what they are: a belated attempt to plug a gap in the general regime of enforcement of promises, a gap left by the artificial and unfortunate doctrine of consideration. See chapter 3 infra and Fuller and Eisenberg, supra note 25, at 159-161.

agreed, let us suppose the express company could show that the contemplated exhibit would have been a disaster and that the stove company was much better off never having shown at the fair. Perhaps in such a case there should be no award of reliance damages, but should the express company be allowed to keep the prepayment? Should it be able to argue that the stove company is lucky there was a breach?

In terms of both expectation and harm the stove company should get nothing. Its expectation is shown to be negative, and it suffered no harm. And yet it is entirely clear that Railway Express should make restitution. They did nothing for the money and should not keep it. But is this enforcing the promise? Not at all.

V. I owe my plumber ten dollars, so I place a ten-dollar bill in an envelope, which I mistakenly address and send to you.

On what theory can I get my ten dollars back from you? You made no promise to me. You have *done* me no wrong, and so that is not the ground of my demand that you return the money—though you wrong me now if you do not accede to my demand. The principle is a general one: It is wrong to retain an advantage obtained without justification at another's expense. And what justification can you offer for keeping the ten dollars?*[31] What justification can Railway Express offer for keeping the freight charges in case IV? That it has done the stove company a favor by spoiling the exhibit? But this is no favor the stove company asked for and not one that Railway Express had a right to thrust on it. And surely Railway Express cannot say it received the money properly under a contract, since it has utterly repudiated that contract. The contract drops out leaving Railway Express without a justification. In this state of affairs the stove company wins.

Promise and restitution are distinct principles. Neither derives from the other, and so the attempt to dig beneath promise in order to ground contract in restitution (or reliance, for that matter) is misconceived. Contract is based on promise, but when something goes wrong in the contract process—when people fail to reach agreement, or break their promises—there will usually be gains and losses to sort out. The *Red Owl* case is one illustration. Here is another:

*That you thought it was a present, spent it, and would now have to dip into the grocery budget to pay me back? Well, that might be a justification if it were true.

I. Britton signs on to work for Turner for a period of one year at an agreed wage of $120 to be paid at the end of his service. After nine months of faithful service he quits without justification, and Turner without difficulty finds a replacement for him.

On one hand Britton has not kept his promise; on the other Turner has had a substantial benefit at his expense.[32] The promise and restitution principles appear to point in opposite directions in this situation. In chapter 8 I consider at length the way these two principles work together, when and why one or the other of them has priority. For the present it is sufficient to note that it is the very distinctness of the principles that causes such questions to arise. Certainly nothing about the promise principle, the conception of contract as promise, entails that all disputes between people who have tried but failed to make a contract or who have broken a contract must be decided solely according to that principle.

# 3

# CONSIDERATION

 It is a standard textbook proposition that in Anglo-American law a promise is not binding without consideration. Consideration is defined as something either given or promised in exchange for a promise.[1] As it stands this proposition is too unqualified to be quite accurate. Into the nineteenth century a promise contained in a document bearing a seal was binding without consideration in most common law jurisdictions. In the last hundred years there has been a gradual movement to abolish the effect of the seal by legislation,[2] while statutes in different jurisdictions have made a wide variety of particular promises binding without consideration: promises to keep an offer open,[3] to release a debt,[4] to modify an obligation,[5] to pay for past favors.[6] Nevertheless, the trend away from the seal as an anachronistic relic and the narrow, episodic nature of the statutory exceptions leaves the doctrine of consideration as very much the norm.

It is the doctrine of consideration that leads some to see contract as distinct from promise; it is consideration that leads people to say that promise may be all well and good as a ground of moral obligation, but the law is concerned with different and more serious business.[7] What is this more serious business? One intuitive idea is that exchanges are enforced because one who welches on an exchange is a kind of cheat or thief: He has obtained a benefit and now refuses to pay for it. As we have seen in chapter 2, this intuitive sense does not fit the facts—at least in the many cases of executory contracts where the "cheat" has not yet received anything in exchange for his promise except the "victim's" own promise. Where you have given in exchange for my promise nothing more than your own return promise, it is a bootstrap argument to reason that you must be allowed to recover because I by my breach appropriate to myself a value without rendering the agreed-upon exchange. The only value I have received or you given is just your promise, and so I benefit at your expense only on the premise that your promise is enforceable. But that premise is inadmissible in an argument designed to show that promises are enforceable only so far as necessary to prevent one party from deriving a one-sided benefit. This is not to say that exchanges of promises are not truly exchanges, only that the prevention of unjust enrichment cannot be the basis for enforcing such promissory exchanges. An analogous argument obtains to block the suggestion that the doctrine of consideration shows that the law of contracts is concerned not to enforce promises but to compensate harm suffered through reliance.

Exactly what kind of challenge does the doctrine of consideration pose to my thesis of contract as promise? If consideration implies a basis other than promise for contractual obligation, what exactly is that basis? To answer these questions and thus take the measure of the challenge, we must examine the present doctrine in some detail. The doctrine comprises two propositions: (A) The consideration that in law promotes a mere promise into a contractual obligation is something, or the promise of something, given in exchange for the promise. (B) The law is not at all interested in the adequacy of the consideration. The goodness of the exchange is for the parties alone to judge—the law is concerned only that there *be* an exchange.[8] Thus the classic conception seeks to affirm both exchange and freedom of contract. These two ideas turn out to be contradictory.

Consider first the leading case of *Hamer v. Sidway:*[9]

    I. An uncle promises his nephew that he will pay him $5000 if the nephew will neither smoke nor drink until his twenty-first birthday. The nephew complies, but the uncle's executor refuses to pay, claiming the promise was made without consideration.

The court held that the nephew's forbearance was sufficient consideration, even if the nephew had benefited from this forbearance and indeed even if the nephew had had no desire to smoke or drink in that period. It was enough that he had the right to do so and did not exercise it. The law will not inquire into actual motives. This seems reasonable. Imagine a concert manager refusing to pay a pianist an agreed fee on the ground that the pianist would have been glad to perform for nothing. Such subjective inquiries are obviously objectionable. How then should we deal with this case:

    II. A father, wanting to assure his son of a gift but not having the funds in hand, promises to pay $5000 in return for a peppercorn or some other worthless object.[10]

Such a promise, we are told, is unenforceable because the peppercorn is "a mere pretense."[11] When the law says that there must be an exchange, it means just that and not a charade pretending to be an exchange. This too seems reasonable, but how can we decide that the exchange in this case is a charade without looking either at motive—which *Hamer* forbids us to do—or at the substance of the exchange, which the second of the two premises (B) stated at the outset of this section forbids?

    The concept of exchange is highly abstract. Perhaps the inquiry would be advanced if we used the more evocative term "bargain,"[12] which is in fact traditionally used to explain consideration. To this we may add Holmes's suggestion that consideration does not necessarily require an actual bargain, but "reciprocal *conventional* inducement."[13] This means either a real bargain *or* the kind of exchange that in general constitutes an actual bargain, though in a particular case the usual motive might be missing. People do not usually exchange large sums of money for peppercorns, but they regularly bargain about the terms of compensation for a musical performance. How else, after all, are pianists supposed to make a living? Thus the suggestion is that a transaction counts as a bargain either if it was so intended or if it belongs to a type of transactions that people generally bargain about. It looks as if the law can then go about its business of enforcing promissory exchanges without having to look at their substance—that is, allowing people the freedom to make whatever bargains seem best to them. If the doctrine of consideration did at least this the only question left to answer would be what there is about bargains that makes them among promises the privileged objects of legal recognition.

An examination of some cases shows, however, that this simple notion depending on the intuitive idea of bargain cannot account for all of the epicycles of the doctrine of consideration.

III. An author promises his agent that the agent will have the exclusive right to deal with his manuscript during six months, in return for the agent's adding the manuscript to his list. The agent does not promise to make any effort at all to place the manuscript, but he does insist that without the exclusive right he will do nothing.

The common law holds that a promisor in the author's position is not bound, because the agent has given no consideration—he has promised nothing in return for the author's promise, nor paid for the exclusive privilege of considering the manuscript.[14] Yet there is a bargain in the sense that the author has obtained something he wants—namely, the *chance* that this agent might peddle his manuscript—something he could not have obtained other than in return for his promise. And in general the common law has refused to admit the enforceability of options, unless the beneficiary has given or promised something of value for the option. Such arrangements are said to lack mutuality.[15]

Lack of mutuality is only one ground for denying enforcement to arrangements that are bargains in fact. Here is another:

IV. A widow promises to repay a debt owed by her deceased husband in return for the creditor bank's canceling the estate's debt. The husband's estate is without assets, and no part of the canceled debt could ever have been collected.

Is there not consideration for the widow's promise? Let us assume the widow knows that the released claim is worthless. Nevertheless she considers the prospect of clearing her husband's name worth exchanging for a promise to pay the debt. Is this not a bargain? We can even imagine the bank and the widow actually haggling about the details of the promise. Yet the court said that since the bank gave nothing of value, the widow's promise was unenforceable.*[16] The widow believed she was "buying" something of value to her, so this is not even a case of a pretended bargain. Perhaps the court found the transaction too far from the central paradigm of a bargain, too remote from the model of some standard commercial transaction; but if so, case III is hard to explain. Perhaps, then, the court had a sense that the widow was being put upon in a difficult situation; but such transactions have been held to lack consideration even where no widows are involved, while plenty of hard bargains made by distressed widows are enforced.

Consider this case:

> V. A small contractor borrows money from one of his craftsmen and becomes bankrupt without repaying it. Many years later, he makes an explicit written promise to pay this debt, even though it has long ago become unenforceable by reason of both the bankruptcy and the passage of time.

In this case courts typically do enforce the subsequent promise, using the puzzling rationale that the prior obligation is somehow sufficient to support a later promise—the passage of time and the bar of bankruptcy being held to be only formal defects which the subsequent promise removes.[17] Whatever the substantive merit of allowing recovery in such cases, the stated explanation is obviously gibberish. To be consistent the courts would have to find that in such cases there was no bargain, any more than in the case of the widow, since one does not bargain for what one already has: the repentant contractor has already got clear of all obligation the money that he subsequently promises to repay. This notion that you cannot bargain for what you already have is illustrated in these so-called moral consideration cases:

> VI. A workman throws himself in the way of a falling object, saving his employer's life but suffering disabling injuries. The grateful employer promises a pension, which the employer's executors refuse to continue, on the grounds that it was promised without consideration.

*Cases where a person exacts a promise by threat to bring baseless litigation can be dealt with under the doctrine of duress. See chapter 7 infra.

VII. A family nurses to health over a considerable period the adult son of a distant father. When the father learns of this kindness, he promises recompense but does not keep his promise.

In the second of these cases the court accepted the consequences of the bargain theory and refused enforcement.[18] In the first that result was apparently too repellent to accept and the court granted enforcement — by a process of reasoning too strained to repeat.[19] But the problem of promises about prior obligations may arise as well in contexts where not gratitude but calculation is the motive:

VIII. Architect threatens to abandon supervision of an industrial construction project at a crucial stage unless the desperate owner promises to pay an additonal fee.[20]

IX. Builder discovers that the land on which he has contracted to build consists of a shallow crust of hard earth with swamp underneath. Completing the project would be far more costly than he had expected. Although the builder clearly accepted the risk of such a surprise, the owner promises to pay an additional sum on successful completion of the work.[21]

X. Debtor is hard pressed and promises to pay creditor an already overdue debt in three montly installments in return for creditor's promise to forgive the promised interest on the debt.[22]

In each of these cases, the promisor later reneges. Owners in cases VIII and IX claim that they received nothing for their promises and so refuse the extra payment. In the first of these the defense succeeded and the architect did not recover; in the second the defense failed and builder recovered. The creditor in X later claims the interest on the debt on the ground that debtor paid nothing for creditor's promise to forgive the interest. The common law has regularly enforced the original debt in full against the debtor in spite of the creditor's promise of partial forgiveness.[23]

The bargain theory of consideration not only fails to explain why this pattern of decisions is just; it does not offer *any* consistent set of principles from which all of these decisions would flow. These cases particularly cannot be accounted for by the two guiding premises of the doctrine of consideration: (A) that only promises given as part of a bargain are enforceable; (B) that whether there is a bargain or not is a formal question only. As in the cases of the author and the widow (III and IV), so in each of these cases there has been a bargain in fact: The owners and creditor have promised something in return for an assurance or performance. The difference is that in cases VIII-X there is a unilateral modification of earlier bargains so that the promisors (the two owners and the creditor) make new promises, but get no more (creditor gets *less*) than they were entitled to under their old bargains. Nevertheless, new bargains have been made, and propositions A and B are satisfied.[24]

The intuitive appeal of the decisions, at least in the two building cases, VIII and IX, may be easily explained. Architect has owner over a barrel: Their original bargain made owner depend on him, and the second bargain exploits the vulnerability created by the owner's trust in that original promise. The builder in IX, by contrast, has had a nasty surprise, though by the terms of the original deal the risk of such a surprise was his. Finally, case X may be one where debtor, like the builder, falls on unexpected difficulties, or it may be more like IX: exploitation of the creditor's unwillingness to suffer the expense and hazards of suing for his money.

The formal device to deal with these modification cases is the doctrine that consideration not only must be bargained for but must be "fresh"—that the promisor cannot, as it were, sell the same thing twice.[25] So perhaps we might just add to A and B a new premise, A': that what is given or promised in return for a promise must not be something that is already owed to the promisor. Never mind for a moment why we are adding this premise, ask only if now the courts can proceed formally—that is, in compliance with premise B—to decide which promises are to be enforced. This new theory of consideration (consisting now of three propositions) would certainly block the blackmailing architect in VIII, but only at the cost of blocking the quite reasonable accommodation between the builder and the owner in IX. And it offers no way to distinguish reasonable from extortionate compositions between debtors and creditors. (The common law does indeed fail to make that distinction, applying it indiscriminately to all debtor compositions.)

The rigors of this expanded theory might be mitigated if we treated a contract modification as if builder and owner in IX had cancelled their old contract and entered into a new one containing the desired additional compensation for builder. At the time of the modification each still owed the other some duty under the old contract (builder to build; owner to pay). Without looking at motives and content (premise B), we can treat the putative mutual release of these outstanding obligations as a bargain, and having done so the way is clear to the making of a new bargain on whatever terms the parties choose.[26] Neat? Alas, it is not to be. For if the trick works in case IX where we want it to, it will work in VIII too, where we do not. If we exclude the trick in both, A' bars too much; if we allow it in both, whatever we hoped to accomplish by A' is circumvented. And if we allow it only where the purpose is "reasonable" or the new arrangement fair on its merits, we violate B. Indeed the situation is worse still: The trick will not work at all for any case like X, reasonable or not. At the time debtor and creditor contemplate a modification, the only outstanding obligation is the debtor's, so there can be no *mutual* release of obligations, no mutual bargain to tear up the old contract. (In a case like X the debtor would have to offer some actual fresh consideration.) But some cases like X will be as appealing as IX or as unappealing as VIII, yet none can be accommodated.

I conclude that the standard doctrine of consideration, which is illustrated by the preceding ten quite typical common law cases, does not pose a challenge to my conception of contract law as rooted in promise, for the simple reason that that doctrine is too internally inconsistent to offer an alternative at all. The matrix of the inconsistency is just the conjunction of propositions A and B. Proposition B affirms the liberal principle that the free arrangements of rational persons should be respected. Proposition A, by limiting the class of arrangements to bargains, holds that individual self-determination is not a sufficient ground of legal obligation, and so implies that collective policies may after all override individual judgments, frustrating the projects of promisees after the fact and the potential projects of promisors. Proposition A is put forward as if it were neutral after all, leaving the parties their "freedom of contract." But there is a sense in which any promisor gets something for his promise, if only the satisfaction of being able to realize his purpose through the promise. Freedom of contract *is* freedom of promise, and, as my illustrations show, the intrusions of the standard doctrines of consideration can impose substantial if random restrictions on perfectly rational projects.

The anomalous character of the doctrine of consideration has been widely recognized. A variety of statutes abrogate some of its more annoying manifestations, such as the unenforceability of gratuitous options or of contract modifications. There have also been proposals for its virtual abolition.* Before commenting on these proposals briefly at the end of this chapter, I must turn to a perspective on the doctrine that rescues it from its gravest anomalies and does indeed pose a challenge to my view.

In a recent work, John Dawson compares the common law to French and German law and concludes that an impulse shared by all of these systems distinguishes gratuitous promises, that is, promises to make a gift, from true bargains.[27] Another comparativist, Arthur von Mehren, writing in *The International Encyclopedia of Comparative Law*,[28] also contrasts bargains to promises to make a gift, dubbing the latter economically "sterile."[29] Dawson faults the common law not for making this distinction, but for assuming "a doctrinal overload" in using the doctrine of consideration to regulate or exclude promises that hold an offer open (options) and promises that modify or discharge existing arrangements. Dawson emphasizes what he believes is the basic idea of the doctrine of consideration, the substantive, intuitive idea of bargain. Options and modifications fall under that notion because they are part of a "deal"; they are related to bargains. An option is the first step along the way to a bargain. Cases like VIII-X also occur as part of the bargaining process; modifications and discharges should be facilitated to keep that process flexible and serviceable. Substantive unfairness should be controlled not by the manipulation of formalities but by substantive inquiry under the aegis of the doctrines of duress and unconscionability.

This conception challenges my thesis that the basis of contract is promise by locating that basis now in a distinct collective policy, the furtherance of economic exchange.[30] A promise may be necessary, on this view, but it is the largely commercial needs of the market that ground contract. As an explanation this is certainly more satisfying than the incoherent formalities of the common law doctrine, but it too fails on inspection. Neither Dawson's proposal nor French and German law limits contract to commercial transactions: Deals between private individuals selling or exchanging property in no recognized or customary market and family settlements of many

---

*The most striking of these are Samuel Williston's Model Written Obligations Act (in force only in Pennsylvania) and Lord Wright's call, as yet unanswered, in "Ought the Doctrine of Consideration to Be Abolished from the Common Law?," 49 *Harv. L. Rev.* 1225 (1936). Though he disapproves, Professor Atiyah quite correctly observes that these calls are the logical entailments of freedom of contract and the promise principle. Atiyah, supra note 8, at 134-40, 440, 452-54, 687-90; and see Fried, review of Atiyah, 93 *Harv. L. Rev.* 1858, 1865-67 (1980).

sorts are everywhere recognized as binding. It could hardly be otherwise, for to deny a private individual the facility for, say, selling his car or his house to a friend, would lessen the free transferability of property and thus its value, while creating a wholly unjustifiable monopoly in some vaguely defined merchant class. So apparently at least these transactions are not economically "sterile." Rather it is agreed all around that the gift, the donative promise, is the villain of the piece, because of its "sterility." But why is my enforceable promise to sell my brother-in-law my automobile less sterile than my promise to give it to my nephew? The law recognizes the *completed* transaction (after I actually hand over or sign over the automobile), presumably in recognition of my right to do with my property as I choose. In a sense the completed transaction in both cases is quite fertile enough: It is an expression of my will, it increases my satisfaction in some broad sense, and it does so by increasing the satisfaction of my nephew or brother-in-law. Both actual transfers are useful just in the sense that any freely chosen, significant act of mine is useful to me, and therefore is of net utility to society unless it harms someone else. Allowing people to *make* gifts (let us assume freely, deliberately, reasonably) serves social utility by serving individual liberty.*[31] Given the preceding chapter's analysis of promise, there simply are no grounds for not extending that conclusion to *promises* to make gifts. I make a gift because it pleases me to do so. I promise to make a gift because I cannot or will not make a present transfer, but still wish to give you a (morally and legally) secure expectation.

I conclude that the life of contract is indeed promise, but this conclusion is not exactly a statement of positive law. There are too many

*The objection might be raised that in the case of the promise to make a gift my account of the moral basis for promissory obligation does not hold: It is not obvious that a disappointed promisee, who has suffered no losses in reliance on the promise, is "used" or his confidence "abused" when he is not given a promised gift. And yet abuse there is. The promisor for reasons of his own has chosen to create in the promisee what is, by hypothesis, a firm expectation fixed in moral obligation. The promisee thinks he has something — a moral entitlement — which is what the promisor wants him to think he has. And now, having created this expectation, the promisor chooses to disappoint it. Consider an analogous case drawn from the morality of lying: I tell you that I have just heard you have been awarded the Nobel Prize in philosophy. One hour later, before you have had a chance to spend the prospective prize money or even to announce this fact, I tell you that the whole thing was a joke. I have lied to you. I have abused your confidence and used you. Now in both this case and the gift-promise case the harm may have been trivial and perhaps the wrong done rather marginal, but that is beside the point. In both instances for analogous reasons I have indeed wronged you.

gaps in the common law enforcement of promises to permit so bold a statement. My conclusion is rather that the doctrine of consideration offers no coherent alternative basis for the force of contracts, while still treating promise as necessary to it. Along the way to this conclusion I have made or implied a number of qualifications to my thesis. The promise must be freely made and not unfair. This is the subject of chapters 6 and 7. It must also have been made rationally, deliberately. The promisor must have been serious enough that subsequent legal enforcement was an aspect of what he should have contemplated at the time he promised.* Finally, certain promises, particularly those affecting the situation and expectations of various family members, may require substantive regulation because of the legitimate interests of third parties. In a classic article, "Consideration as Form,"[32] Lon Fuller argued that the doctrine of consideration serves several, often convergent policies. The law hesitates to enforce casual promises where promisor or promisee or both would be surprised to find the heavy machinery of the law imposed on what seemed an informal encounter. Requiring an exchange increases the chance that the parties had in contemplation serious business with serious consequences. Moreover, by requiring an exchange, the law allows contracts to be channeled into a number of predetermined types of arrangements, and the existence of these types itself alerts the parties to a conventional set of problems to be considered and a conventional set of answers to those problems. Finally, the requirement of an exchange might exclude the more dubious and meretricious kinds of gift in which strangers are promised the moon, to the prejudice of a spouse or children.

According to Fuller these are convergent reasons for requiring consideration, because none is either necessary or sufficient. There is

*This last qualification is captured in the law by the term "intention to create legal relations." The term as it stands is misleading. No one supposes that two merchants who make a deal must entertain some additional intention to create legal relations in order for that deal to be binding in law. On the other hand, given the consensual basis of contract as promise, the parties should in principle be free to *exclude* legal enforcement so long as this is not a fraudulent device to trap the unwary. See, e.g., Spooner v. Reserve Life Insurance, 47 Wash.2d 454, 287, P.2d 735 (1955). In a particular case it may be a difficult problem of interpretation whether such a purpose is fairly to be implied. In a particular case it will be a task for interpretation to determine whether legal enforcement would not do violence to the intention of the parties — as with so-called social promises. See Henry Hart and Albert Sacks, "The Invitation to Dinner Case," *The Legal Process* 477-478 (tentative ed., Cambridge, 1958). And legal enforcement may violate the understanding of one but not the other party. Compare Armstrong v. M'Ghee, Addison 261 (Westmoreland County Ct. Pa. 1795), and chapter 5 infra.

the important category of family settlements, and surely these should not be denied enforceability indiscriminately. Furthermore, by using the correct forms it is possible to cast wholly novel trans-actions—transactions unsupported by the gloss of custom and ex-perience—in an enforceable mold. Finally, the doctrine of con-sideration makes it possible to lend enforceability to arrangements that are trivial if not frivolous, so long as the forms are observed. And indeed, so long as the forms are observed, it is possible that a person who makes a promise will be legally bound even if he did not intend to be legally bound—if he intended only to promise and to take some value in exchange for his promise. Consideration in Fuller's view is like a rather awkward tool, which has the virture of being able to pound nails, drive screws, pry open cans, although it does none of these things well and although each of them might be done much better by a specialized tool. (The archaic institution of the promise under seal might be compared for its ability to serve these useful ends with more or less convenience.)

The movement in the law rather suggests that we may have in the not too distant future a more candid set of principles to determine which promises should be enforceable in terms of the fairness of each type. We are moving in that direction as a result of decisions and statutes lending validity to types of promises whose legitimacy had been in doubt under the doctrine of consideration: option contracts, firm offers, compromises of debts, modification of contracts, and the whole domain of promissory estoppel. Secondly, we are moving in that direction as a result of a more open willingness to stigmatize certain promises as unfair or unconscionable and to deny enforce-ment on that ground rather than on the ground of insufficient con-sideration.[33]

4

# ANSWERING
# A PROMISE

# OFFER AND
# ACCEPTANCE

Contract law is complex. This complexity may seem to count against the thesis that it is grounded in the primitive moral institution of promising, for morality should be available to the ordinary man, in touch with his intuitions, and not require for its understanding the trained ingenuity of a professional. Karl Llewellyn remarked that generations of law students have encountered the intricacies of offer and acceptance in contract law as perhaps their first quintessentially technical body of doctrine.[1] Yet, as I shall argue in this chapter, this body of doctrine relates at least in part to a feature of promising that I have not yet touched upon, a feature that must be explicated before my exposition of promising is complete, and one that the ordinary man will recognize at once: A promise is made *to* someone; it gives the prom-

40

isee a right to expect, to call for its performance; and so by implication a promise, to be complete, to count as a promise, must in some sense be taken up by its beneficiary.

## PROMISES AND VOWS

Imagine that a group of men and women, believing that it is important to hold down population growth, pick out my name at random from the telephone directory and each writes me a postcard promising me to produce no more than two children. Is there not something strange in the proposal that all of these people are now under a promissory obligation *to me* to limit the size of their families?[2] In order to have a third child without violating a duty to me must they really secure a release from me? Consider the imposition on me. I may be quite unclear about the problems of population limitation, so that if some couple's having another child depends on my releasing them from their promise, then perhaps before I do so I will want to look into the facts of their case. Or perhaps I do not believe in population limitation, but feel I have no right to impose my views on others. How can all of this "power" to control others' actions have been thrust upon me against my will? Don't say that since I can simply ignore the problem, nothing has been thrust upon me against my will! How can I ignore the problem? A couple has come to me and asked me to release them from their "obligation." If I simply turn away, what is the situation then? Have I released them or have I not? You might say that by turning away, I have released them. But I may want neither to release them nor *not* to release them. I may just not want to have anything to do with their problem. And don't say that I can always refuse to enforce the promise, or refuse to scold the promisors for breaking it, or even refuse to feel resentment at the breach. The moral force of a promise cannot depend on whether the promisee chooses to "enforce" the promise. After all, what does it mean to enforce a promise in the moral sphere? I suppose one can demand its performance, but if there is a morally binding obligation under a promise, the existence of the obligation does not depend on a demand by the promisee—nor on his scolding the promisor, nor on his feeling resentment.

This admittedly bizarre example shows the need to deepen our initial concept of promising, which failed to distinguish between the usual case of a promise and what one might call a vow. The conception of promising I have developed so far suggests, for instance, that the following might create a morally binding obligation, the obligation of a promise: You say to yourself with great force, feeling, and seriousness that you commit yourself to make a thousand-dollar donation to your local classical music station. Surely there is something odd in saying that you have *promised* to do that. To whom have you promised? Perhaps to God—but this just makes the point that a personal promisee must be posited, a promisee who holds the reins of the obligation. Have you promised to yourself, then? If to yourself, then you are free to release yourself in the same way that any other promisee may. When it comes time for performance you may release yourself on whatever grounds would have been morally sufficient for not making a contribution at that (later) time in the absence of a promise. A promise to oneself adds nothing to the moral grounds for making the contribution absent the promise. One thing seems clear: You have not made a promise to the radio station, since you have not communicated with it. So what is missing, what is this additional element that transforms a vow or a commitment to oneself into a promise to another? If the radio station had given consideration, the element of bargain or exchange would certainly promote your commitment from a mere vow to a promise. As we have seen in the preceding chapter, however, an exchange is necessary neither to promissory nor to (a correct view of) contractual obligation. What the exchange (consideration) accomplishes is to supply some other truly necessary element. Perhaps this is why it has seemed so natural to insist on consideration. The fact that I pay for a promise establishes two things: that the promise was made *to* me, and that I desired the promise to be made.

The case of the vow shows that a promise is something essentially communicated to someone—to the promisee, in the standard case.[3] (In the next section I deal with the nonstandard case where the addressee of the promise may not seem to be its beneficiary.) A promise is relational; it invokes trust, and so its communication is essential. But my hypothetical case of the "promise" to bear only two children shows that communication is not enough. A promise cannot just be thrust on someone—he must in some sense be willing to be its beneficiary.* This additional element might in a very general way be

---

*An even stronger case, discussed in the philosophical literature, is the threat couched in promissory form: "If you don't pay up, I'll break your legs—and that's a promise." The use of the word promise may lend emphasis, but hardly places the threatener

identified as the requirement that the promise benefit the promisee. This suggestion, however, fails to bring out that some promises may propose a benefit to the promisee that the promisee does not want, or does not want from this promisor. Now it might be said that if the promisee does not want the promise, it cannot count as a benefit *to him*, but this makes the notion of benefit unilluminating. Moreover, it may not be the thing promised that he does not want, nor even that thing from that promisor, but rather he may not want it *as a promise*. The family-limitation example again illustrates this point. These difficulties are met if we identify as a further necessary condition of promissory obligation *that the promise be accepted*.

The need for acceptance shows the moral relation of promising to be voluntary on both sides. It is part of the intuitive force behind the idea of exchange. And acceptance offers a further point of correspondence between the moral institution of promise and the legal insititution of contract. I admit unease, however, about insisting on acceptance in the case where the promise is clearly communicated and where it would be captious to doubt that the promisee is delighted by the promise. Yet I stick to the conception of promising as requiring acceptance. Since, as we have seen, any putative benefit may in fact be unwanted by a particular (putative) promisee, there must at least be the option to refuse or reject not just the benefit but the promise of the benefit. But it may be an imposition even to put a putative promisee in a situation in which unless he speaks up and refuses this unwanted relation is thrust on him. In many situations, if I look you in the eye and promise you one thousand dollars, your acceptance may readily be inferred from the circumstances. I infer it, you infer that I infer it, and so on. So rather than jettison the requirement of acceptance, I suggest that in such cases we recognize that there is tacit acceptance,[4] admitting only that sometimes the line between tacit acceptance and a mere willingness to receive a promise may be exceedingly hard to draw. What marks that line in principle is the set of mutual tacit inferences of acceptance referred to above.

---

under a moral obligation to break his victim's legs, or gives the victim a right that his legs be broken. See Pall Ardal, "And That's a Promise," 18 *Phil Q.* 225 (1968); Vera Peetz, "Promises and Threats," 86 *Mind* (n.s.) 578 (1977): "a promise is a pledge to do something for you, not to you," quoting John Searle, *Speech Acts* (Cambridge, England, 1969).

## ACCEPTANCE AND THE LAW OF
## THIRD-PARTY BENEFICIARIES

There is a class of cases in which a binding promise is made and yet the beneficiary may never even learn of it. In there cases A promises B (let us assume for good consideration) that A will render a benefit to C. Does the recognition of promissory obligation in such cases refute my thesis about the necessity of acceptance? This theoretical question is the subject of an involved body of contract doctrine, the law of third-party beneficiaries. The exploration of that doctrine illuminates the theoretical inquiry.

One response that might be made is that this case is not, after all, like a vow or an uncommunicated promise, since there are a standard promisor (A) and a standard promisee (B). Though C did not accept the promise, B did. Consequently A is at least bound to B, and the fact that what A is bound to is to render a performance to C seems irrelevant to the issue at hand. (It is as if A promised B to build a monument to B's dead cat.) And this indeed is how the law was originally inclined to look at the matter. But persistent problems arose: (1) If B is the promisee, what is C's standing to enforce the promise? For a long time the law held that only B could sue, with the inconvenience that, since often B suffered no injury from a breach, B could recover only nominal damages.[5] Ways around this difficulty were found, and finally C was allowed to sue in his own name for the benefit promised by A.[6] But this solution itself led to problems that illustrate the theoretical issue before us: (2) If B is the promisee, should B not be able to release A for any reason he chooses, just as he can release A in the event of a promise to benefit B himself? Why should C be heard to complain if A and B, having gotten together to confer a benefit on C, now get together again and change their minds? On this issue the law has long been in confusion. According to one solution B may not release A after C has *relied* to his detriment on A's promise. But this begs the question. As we have seen, not every act of reliance creates an obligation, but only reliance that is somehow justified. And what justifies C here in relying on A's promise? Should C not have to count on the possibility that A and B might agree to revoke the benefit they had decided to confer on him?

A sensible response to these difficulties recognizes that there will be situations in which what A and B are trying to do—the very purpose of their arrangement — is to create some right, some firm expectation in C. There must be situations in which A and B want to do for C what promissors and promisees generally want to do for each other: to tie down the future by way of moral obligation. But the logic of the argument that allows promisor and promisee to undo the bonds that they themselves have tied would seem to prevent them from conferring an irrevocable benefit on C, though conferring an irrevocable benefit may be just what they want to do. In order to make it possible for A and B to accomplish this, the law has concluded that not only reliance but also C's "acceptance" of the promise will cause C's rights to vest, preventing A and B from undoing what they have done.[7] This legal doctrine shows acceptance in its purest form, untinctured by any element of counterpromise or exchange. It is the very operative act of acquiescing in the promissory benefit that I have argued is necessary to complete a binding promise. (I concede that in Anglo-American law this operative act of acceptance is found in its pure form only in C's, the third party's, acceptance; the promisee, B, must not only accept but give consideration. In continental law pure acceptance is operative in two-party as well as third-party contracts.)[8] Sometimes it is said that accepting makes C a party to the contract; his acceptance makes it as if the promise had been made to him. And of course he can accept only if somehow or other, directly or indirectly, he gets wind of the promise. Before C's acceptance, A's promise to B is, as far as C is concerned, more like a vow than a promise.*

## THE SIMPLE CIRCUITRY OF OFFER AND ACCEPTANCE

Promises — and therefore contracts — are fundamentally relational; one person must make the promise to another, and the second person must accept it. Acceptance may be assured by any conventional

*Public offers of rewards pose this special perplexity in the law: does a person who fulfills the terms of the reward "accept" the offer, even though he never knew of the offer until after his performance was completed? If the answer is yes, then we have the anomaly of a promise being accepted by someone who did not know he was accepting. If the answer is no, practical problems of administration arise, particularly the invitation to perjury on the part of the claimant. Yet it is not just practical problems that make it seem unjust to deny the claimant his reward. Should we say that the offer was made to the "public," of which the claimant is a member? Though this seems an artificial solution it does mark the fact that the promise was hardly a private one, as in the case of the vow. Not surprisingly, different jurisdictions have reached different conclusions. See Vitty v. Eley, 51 App. Div. 44, 64 N.Y.S. 397 (1900); von Mehren, note 4 supra.

device, such as speaking the words "I accept" with the intention of referring to a conventional device in which the words figure. There are wide latitude and informality in what counts as an intention to accept a promise, just as the promise itself can be made in many ways.[9] The intuitive force behind the doctrine of consideration comes to the fore in those promises where the promisor himself requires not only acceptance of his undertaking but a return of some sort. Of course we must distinguish the case where the promisor merely expects or hopes for some return from the case where he *conditions* his promise on that return. In the latter case, if the return is not forthcoming he is not just disappointed; he can claim that the obligation of his promise never came into existence.*

The principle of expanding human liberty by recognizing the self-imposed obligation of promises also entails that a man be able to condition his promise on receiving a return from the promisee. And of course there is no reason to exclude conditional promises a priori as a class or to ignore the condition. Nevertheless only in the nineteenth century were conditional promises fully recognized and their terms respected. This development in the law was, I suspect, associated with the development of the law of offer and acceptance at that time. As I will show, the concepts of conditional promises and of offer and acceptance are closely related in principle as well as in history.[10]

A wishes to be bound to B by a promissory obligation x, but only if B will be bound to him by promissory obligation y. (Of course A's ultimate purpose is to get y from B, and becoming bound to B for x is A's chosen means for obtaining y.) A promises x to B, if B will promise y to A. A's conditional promise is called in law the offer, B's the acceptance. B's promise serves three overlapping functions: (1) It sat-

---

*A different question is this: what if A conditions his promise not on B's performance, but on his promise: if you will promise to mow my lawn for the next five years I promise to shovel your drive for the same period. The first winter arrives and I perform, but comes spring you do not. Strictly speaking, this is different from the problem in the text since I got what I demanded—your return promise. Now for that reason do I have to go on shoveling your drive for the next four winters, perhaps suing you for the cost of finding a substitute gardener, or may I withdraw with legal and moral impunity? In other words, does your breaking your promise cancel my reciprocal obligation to you or just give me a remedy for my disappointment? There is no obvious a priori reason for one or the other response. It does seem fairer to release someone from an obligation of trust to another who has shown himself unwilling to accept the same obligation. This solution was not settled law until the nineteenth century. Before that time it seems that the victim of a breach was not released from his reciprocal obligation, but had to rely on a suit for damages for relief. I discuss conditions at greater length in chapter 8 infra.

isfies the condition in A's offer.* (2) It is "acceptance" in the general sense that all promissory obligation is reciprocal and so all promises must be accepted, even unconditional ones. (3) It furnishes the consideration that the Anglo-American law generally requires to make a promise legally binding. From this simple concept of offer and acceptance a number of increasingly intricate consequences flow.

Where the promise is conditional, as in my schematic example, until the condition is fulfilled A is not bound in law by the obligation of a promise. An unaccepted offer may be retracted at any time. Imagine that B answers A's offer in this way: I accept your promise, but I will not promise you y. This (let us call it) naked acceptance is wholly without legal or moral effect.[11] To bind A on the basis of such an "acceptance," without his condition being met, is to bind him to an obligation he did not undertake and thus is to do violence to the principle of enlarging liberty by enforcing promises. Indeed it seems more accurate to say that B has not accepted A's promise at all; he has accepted a promise that A might have made or that B wishes A had made, but not the one A in fact made. Let us express this by saying that a promisor should be able to control what counts as acceptance of his promise. (In law there is the saying that the offeror is "master of the bargain.") But if B has not accepted the promise then A is not bound by it, and if not bound he is free—free to withdraw his offer.[12] This is the altogether rational idea behind the doctrine that an offeror—or conditional promisor, as I call him—is free to retract his offer at any time prior to acceptance, at any time before his condition is met. Why should he not be? His promise has not been accepted and thus cannot bind him *as a promise* (although, as we shall see, it may bind him in other ways and for other reasons).

Consider the force of a promise to be an electric current. For the current to flow, the circuit must be completed. There are two switches, the promisor's and the promisee's. If the promisor has closed his switch he is in a situation of vulnerability: The circuit placing him under an obligation can be closed by an act of acceptance by the promisee. But should the promisor reopen his switch before the acceptance, the acceptance by itself is insufficient to complete the circuit.

*Judith Thomson points out (in an unpublished manuscript) that to avoid difficulties the conditional promise-offer should be construed like the statement "If nominations are in order, I nominate Jones." If nominations are indeed in order, I need not go on to nominate Jones; I have already nominated him. So also if you accept my offer, I have eo ipso promised.

47

Can the promisor not obligate himself to keep his switch closed? Of course, but not by the offer-promise alone, for *that* must be accepted. He may, however, make *another* promise, a different, subsidiary promise, to keep his principal promise open (or his principal switch closed). This the law calls an option or a firm offer. But this subsidiary promise must itself be accepted. The common law's mistaken equation of consideration with acceptance has led to the unfortunate doctrine that not only acceptance but consideration is required to make an option binding.[13] (There are, of course, options that by their terms must be paid for. Unless and until paid for, such options are not binding and may be withdrawn. Once they are paid for, even the common law has no problem enforcing them by keeping the principal offer open.) The correct analysis of the gratuitous option requires only simple acceptance of the option (the only acceptance the promisor has asked for). This acceptance would keep the principal offer alive (though not itself complete the principal circuit) for as long as the option provides, so that during that period the promisor could not retract his promise, could not reopen his switch, and so would remain liable to have the circuit completed by the promisee on whatever terms the promise defined. (As I indicated in chapter 3, the inconveniences of the common law rule for options are so manifest that it has been abrogated by a wide variety of statutes.)

Where the promisor specifies acceptance by a counterpromise, that counterpromise all by itself closes the circuit of promissory obligation. Does this mean that counterpromises are an exception to my claim that a promise must be accepted to be binding? Not at all.[14] The counterpromise too must be accepted to be binding; but the offer-promise includes a commitment to accept the offeree's counterpromise, so that that counterpromise both accepts the original offer and triggers the offeror's acceptance of the counterpromise. To be sure, acceptance must be an act — however implicit or minimal — and so it is in this case: an act of commitment to accept the acceptance when it is made. This condition is fulfilled by the offeree and the acceptance becomes unconditional. Nor can I decline to accept your counterpromise when it is communicated to me. Because of my original promise I am bound to accept your counterpromise. By what am I bound? By my original promise, which is made binding by your acceptance. Only by withdrawing before that acceptance of yours do I again become free to decline to accept your counterpromise, your acceptance.

## REJECTIONS, COUNTEROFFERS, CONTRACTS AT A DISTANCE, CROSSED OFFERS

The circuit metaphor allows the elucidation of some persistent puzzles. Take the case of counteroffers. If I offer (promise) to sell you my cow for $100 and you respond that you will (promise to) buy the cow for that sum but only if I throw in a chicken, the common law analysis holds that

> You have not accepted my offer.
> You have made me a counteroffer.
> Your counteroffer acts as a *rejection* of my offer.
> Since you have rejected my offer it is dead; you can no longer accept it unless I first renew it.
> I may accept that counteroffer, concluding the bargain on your terms.

Thus a rejection by the promisee reopens the first switch, so that the promisee's subsequent acceptance is ineffective to complete the circuit.[15] But why not require the offeror to withdraw the offer explicitly, why not allow an offeree to accept any offer until it is withdrawn—even after he has first rejected it? I think there are no reasons in principle, nothing entailed by the concepts themselves, only considerations of fairness and convenience. Recall the vulnerability of my situation after I have made an offer: An obligation can be imposed on me by your act of acceptance alone. I am in your power. To have spoken first in the process of bargaining is a certain disadvantage, though someone must speak first. The balance of advantage is partially restored by requiring you either to accept my offer in its exact terms or to run the risk of being without a bargain and having to make an offer yourself if you want to keep the bargaining going. Otherwise it would be too easy for you to play with me: you could try this and that, and if you sensed I was about to lose patience and withdraw altogether, you could always close the deal by giving the initially specified acceptance after all.*

*If the rule were to the contrary, a promisor might nevertheless achieve the effect of the present rule by explicitly conditioning his offer. Just as I might condition my offer of the $100 cow on your accepting by noon tomorrow, so the principle of liberty dictates that I should be able to condition my offer in other ways—for example, to say that my offer will lapse if you reject it or make a counteroffer. Since it is likely that the offer will often want to impose such conditions, the law makes the rule run that way. After all, an offeror can always specify that rejections will *not* cause his offer to lapse in the rare event that that is his wish. (An offeree might also specify that his counteroffer

As we have examined offer and acceptance so far, we have been able to assume the receipt of the specified acceptance, because we have imagined the acceptor looking the promisor in the eye and saying "I accept." How do we know even then that the promisor heard, that he understood? Does a certain kind of eye contact, a handshake, somehow confirm to the promisee that the promisor has received the acceptance? And do we indeed assume the need for this confirmation of acceptance? And if such confirmation by the promisor of his receipt of the acceptance is necessary to bind him, then should we not also require receipt of the confirmation by the promisee and a confirmation of *that*, and so on ad infinitum? It might be said that this kind of infinite regress is not necessary, since there is a natural stopping place just after the offeror confirms receipt of the acceptance. At that point the promisor knows he is bound (his confirmation tells us that) and the acceptor knows he (the acceptor) is bound (his acceptance tells us that). But in fact the promisor can know he is bound *before* confirming receipt of the acceptance; he can know he is bound on receiving it, and the acceptor can know *he* is bound on giving his acceptance. Beyond that, whether each can be sure that the other meant what he seemed to mean, or heard what he seemed to hear, is a problem that no amount of confirmation or reconfirmation can solve completely. Philosophers will recognize this as an aspect of familiar problems of language, of meaning, and of other minds: How do we ever know what another person means, or that another person has understood what we mean? We need not await the solution to these nice problems. When A answers B's question in the same language and under ordinary conditions and B seems to understand, we do not worry about whether B actually understands A's answer, nor do we develop elaborate devices to assure that what seems like a successful communication really is one.

The problems in law occur not in direct communications but in communications that take time and use imperfect media. Problems principally occur in contracts by postal correspondence. The usual rule of Anglo-American law (known as the mailbox rule) provides that in such cases a contract is concluded when the acceptance is posted,[16] not when it is received—though the promisor may provide to the contrary. A vast amount of ink has been spilled in the attempt to deduce this rule from the general principles of offer and accep-

is tentative only and that he is keeping my offer under advisement. This keeps my offer alive, but weakens the bargaining force of the offeree's counteroffer.)

50

tance. Christopher Columbus Langdell thought the rule wrong in principle.*[17] For the purposes of this essay this famous conundrum is easily resolved. For a promise to be binding it must be accepted, and how that acceptance is to be conveyed to the promisor, indeed whether it must be communicated to him at all, is something the promisor can specify at the time he makes his offer-promise. What is necessary is that the acceptance be unequivocal and irrevocable, or else it will not close the circuit. In postal or telegraphic communication, there are risks that acceptances will be delayed or will miscarry. The parties should be free to allocate these risks, and a rule of law in this matter—so long as it marks the acceptance by some irrevocable act—is satisfactory so long as it offers just a presumptive allocation of the risk, allowing the parties to reallocate it as they wish.

In the context of a postal system that in the nineteenth century was remarkably swift and reliable, the mailbox rule had the virtue of creating maximum certainty at the earliest point. The promisee knew he had a deal as soon as he posted his acceptance, and he could proceed on that basis without awaiting a confirmation. True, the promisor had to consider the risk that he might be bound to a contract without knowing it, but that is both a lesser and a controllable hardship: The promisor initiates the transaction by making the offer, so he can make enquiries if no answer is forthcoming.[18] And if he does not wish to assume even this burden, he can reverse the law's presumption and require actual receipt of the acceptance as a term of his offer. The contrary presumption—that the contract is complete only on receipt of the acceptance—would leave the promisee in exactly the same doubt about his situation as the mailbox rule leaves the promisor. And the effective date of the obligation would be delayed by that one step without any gain in certainty. (Where the

---

*The objection of principle seems to be this: The contractual allocation of risks is voluntary, but unless acceptance is received there is no completed agreement between the parties—including an agreement to allocate the risks—and so an offeror should never be bound until he receives the acceptance.

There is a fallacy here. It is assumed that the promisor's allocation of risk as to receipt of the promisee's acceptance must be the subject of some completed, separate agreement between them. It is sufficient that the mode of acceptance be designated in the original promise. If that promise is accepted as specified then both the substance of the promise and the allocation of risk are binding. Of course the promisor/offeror must find out about the acceptance eventually if his promise is to have any point. But nothing *requires* that he not be bound without knowing it, though he may not wish to be so bound and may limit his offer to prevent being bound where he has not had notice.

mails are unreliable so that uncertainty looms larger, the contrary rule may be better. So many offerors may take advantage of their right to require receipt of the acceptance, that the law might as well save them the trouble.)

Once we see the mailbox rule as a rule of convenience, allocating the risks in the absence of an allocation by the parties, the various refinements of that rule fall into place. The major refinements have to do with (1) withdrawls of offers, (2) withdrawals of acceptances that overtake previously posted acceptances, and (3) attempted later acceptances that overtake previously posted rejections. The law provides that an offer is not effective until it is actually received, and that an acceptance is effective once the promisee puts it irrevocably out of his hands and on its way to the promisor. It would be odd to provide that the promisor's withdrawal of his offer is effective in a way different from the offer itself. And a rule that put the promisee in the position of thinking he had a contract by virtue of the mailbox rule while depriving him of that contract because a withdrawal of the original offer had been dispatched but not yet received at the time of his acceptance would be almost perversely designed to foster confusion. Similarly but less obviously unfair would be a rule permitting the promisee to overtake his previously dispatched acceptance in order to withdraw it. The mailbox rule has the virtue of fixing — in the face of rare but inevitable accidents — the rights of the parties in as determinate a way as possible at the earliest reasonable point. If a later, overtaking withdrawl of acceptance were effective, the following situation would be possible:

A offers to sell corn to B at $5000 a carload, the current market price. B dispatches his acceptance, the normal postal delay being three days. B knows that if within those three days the price of corn falls he can wire or telephone the withdrawal of his acceptance; if it rises or stays firm he will allow his acceptance to go through.

Instead of enforcing a rule of certainty and a fair allocation of the risks, we would allow the promisee to gamble at the promisor's expense.

Now of course if the offeror receives the *later* rejection first and it contains no reference (as it might not) to an earlier acceptance, the offeror can be badly hurt. He is led to believe that his promise has been rejected and that he is off the hook. Perhaps he sells his goods elsewhere. Then he finds that an effective acceptance had been earlier dispatched. The offeror has made a promise, which is binding only if accepted. Well, has the promisee accepted it or has he not? The promisee has created confusion about this, and plainly he, not the promisor, should bear the burden of that confusion, especially since the promisor has had little chance to protect himself. This may be more a principle of tort than of contract, but as we shall see in chapter 5 in respect to other contractual accidents, that is no reason to allow an innocent party to suffer.[19]

The final puzzle is generated by crossed offers.[20] On Monday A sends B a letter offering him x in return for y. On that same day B sends A a letter offering him y for x. Both letters arrive on Wednesday. It is hard to say that either letter accepts the other's offer, and it seems most natural to me to say that there is no contract, but talismanic phrases like "the meeting of the minds" and "consensus ad idem" suggest that a contract has been concluded. Perhaps the minds have met (whatever that means), but they have not gotten out of their cars to shake hands. I rationalize my intuition this way: On Monday there is certainly no contract, for one can only accept a promise one has received. All that A's and B's letters show on Monday is a mutual willingness to exchange x for y, but acceptance of a promise is not just a frame of mind, a favorable disposition, it is an intentional act making implicit or explicit reference to another's promise. The mailbox rule only refers to acceptances — surely it does not cover letters dispatched even before an offer has been received. And what was not an acceptance nor intended as one on Monday cannot turn into an acceptance on Wednesday.

Consider the inconveniences of a rule holding that a contract is concluded on Wednesday. Neither A nor B knows that the other is in receipt of his letter, so the circumstances that would create the contract are not known to *either* party. In the usual case, if A is the offeror, though he does not know that B has accepted when B dispatches his answer, and though for that reason A is bound before he knows it, at least B is quite sure that he has received A's letter and quite sure as well that he (B) has dispatched an answer, and so B knows that all the circumstances for both of them being bound are satisfied. True, in the crossed-offers case each may surmise on Wednesday that the other is that very day probably opening his letter of offer, but to base a contract on such mutual complementary *surmises* is a dubious proposition. For each might as well wonder whether his letter has been delayed, or whether the other is ill or on a trip and so not in a position to read his mail. And if one party has not received the other's letter it would be unfair to that party to close the contractual circuit, since he does not yet know that what he meant as an offer has been "accepted" by an event that occurred two days before the offer was ever received. It is true that both A and B by sending offers showed themselves willing to take the risk of being contractually bound without knowing it, so perhaps it might be said that holding them bound when each has received the other's letter exposes them to no more risk than they were willing to assume. But to conclude the contract on that basis would at least require the promulgation of a rule to that effect, for the result lacks the intuitive naturalness of the standard offer-and-acceptance case. And if a rule must be promulgated, should it not provide explicitly that one of the parties must take the further step of accepting the other's offer? And what if they both do—creating crossed acceptances? I see no problem about recognizing a contract in the case of crossed acceptances, no problem analogous to that of the crossed offers.

This issue is largely theoretical. If a case of crossed offers should arise today I suppose that A and B would immediately pick up the telephone to straighten out the confusion—which would just show that they did indeed view this as a confusion to be straightened out. Also note that this confusion can scarcely arise in direct communications, but is the artifact of the conventional rules governing contracts concluded by correspondence. In a face-to-face situation, after all, if both parties speak at once and in the same words—in a kind of unintentional duet—an immediate adjustment is possible and will take place. That adjustment is what I ask in the case of bargaining by correspondence.

## RELIANCE ON AN OFFER

The offeror is master of the bargain. He may condition his promise however he chooses. Yet there are situations in which a person to whom an offer is made goes to trouble or expense as a result of receiving the offer, without in the end being able to meet the condition and so bind the promisor. In an earlier day the response to this situation was that the promisee relied at his peril. He took the risk, gambled, and lost, and he should not seek to foist on the promisor a responsibility the promisor did not choose to assume.[21] This harsh response was thought to be required by the very nature of contract, by the principle of liberty. Here are two paradigm cases:

I. A promises to pay B if B will complete a specified task. (B's promise is neither required not desired.) B starts work on the task, but when he is halfway through A changes his mind and retracts the offer.

II. Subcontractor offers to do the electrical work at a certain price to General Contractor, who responds that he may use Sub's offer in calculating his overall bid on the building. General does in fact use Sub's offer in his own bid and wins the building contract, but Sub refuses to do the electrical work at the stated price — arguing that since his offer was never accepted, and since General was never bound to Sub, Sub is likewise free of any obligation.

In case I perhaps there is no contract, but, as we shall see in subsequent chapters, there are other bases for doing justice between the parties: restitution and tort.[22] So, for instance, if the task is the completion of a shed on A's land and A purports to withdraw when the shed is partially built, the principle of restitution requires that A should pay for what he has got. And if B has as yet built nothing, but has gone to considerable expense in assembling a crew and locating materials, the tort principle may be used to procure reimbursement. The intuitive force of the case for restitution shows that the restitution principle is particularly powerful where it applies. The case for a tort remedy, by contrast, is open to debate. B is harmed, but did he not assume this risk? Moreover, unlike the restitution case, A gets nothing out of B's loss. Of course if this were all just a malicious trick on the part of A to do B harm, we would have no difficulty requiring compensation, but where A cancels the deal for some good reason of his own we need to find a handle for saying that he was obliged to take B's losses into account. Nor is this like the cases where the law compensates losses caused by reliance on a promise, since A didn't promise — not unconditionally anyway. At best one can say that A's conditional conduct was conduct he should have foreseen would cause harm if withdrawn, or that his withdrawal was conduct he should have foreseen would cause harm. But if we take that line, the claim for compensation is subject to all the usual tort qualifications regarding reasonableness: Did A have an overriding justifying purpose in withdrawing? And more to the point; was B reasonable in undertaking expense, expecting the expense would be reimbursed? If A makes it quite clear to B at the outset that B acts at his risk and peril and that A feels free to withdraw at any time prior to completion, does that not negate the reasonableness of B's reliance? I should think so — at least absent trickery or bad faith on A's part. This point is nicely illustrated by the case in which a reward is offered to an open class of persons.[23] Those who do not catch the culprit or who fail to find the missing object are not entitled to anything no matter how much they have expended in the search. They took the risk.

Case II presents a different situation. There is potential for grave harm and bitter disappointment here, but not because General relies on a conditional, incomplete, inchoate promise by Sub. Rather the problem in this type of case is caused solely by the pernicious doctrine of consideration. For Sub has made a definite promise to General and General has accepted it in the sense of acknowledging it, assenting to it. And so by the promissory principle Sub should be bound.[24] True, General has not accepted in the technical sense of giving value or binding himself to Sub in return, but the doctrine of consideration, not the promissory principle, requires that additional element.

This discussion of offer and acceptance completes the presentation of the main elements of promissory obligation and of the parallel elements in the law of contracts. What follows is a consideration of the response to things going wrong in the promissory regime: mistaken assumptions, unexpected developments, breaches and failures of one or both parties, the question of unfair or coerced promises. In these questions the promissory principle either does not apply at all or must compete with rival moral principles. The challenge is to show that the promissory principle can hold its own against these rivals, while leaving them room to effect such substantial justice as lies within their particular domains.

# 5

# GAPS

The moral force behind contract as promise is autonomy: the parties are bound to their contract because they have chosen to be. When one or both have chosen by mistake (I deal with deceit in chapter 6) this rationale fails, and yet there is something that at least looks like an agreement — and in some sense it is an agreement, though a mistaken one. Classical contract theory has not dealt well with this problem. Too anxious perhaps to preserve the integrity of promises against encroachments by principles imposed on the parties from outside, classical theory has sought to apply the promise principle here as well, and the result has often lacked intuitive plausibility or even coherence. This failure has been taken as a sign of a general defect in the conception of contract as autonomous ordering. The recourse to collectively determined grounds of resolution — particularly to tort notions — has been taken by the critics to show that such grounds in every case lurk behind the facade of promise.[1] In this chapter I consider why mistake has posed such an embarrassment and propose a solution that leaves intact the theory of contract as promise.

## MISTAKE, FRUSTRATION, AND IMPOSSIBILITY

Traditional doctrine distinguishes two kinds of surprises: mistake, and frustration or impossibility. Mistake relates to a false assumption about how things are at the time of contracting; frustration and impossibility relate to incorrect assumptions about how things will be later, when it comes time to perform.[2] The distinction is illustrated by two parallel cases arising out of contracts to hire, for substantial sums, rooms overlooking the route of King Edward VII's coronation procession in 1902. The coronation was postponed because of the king's sudden illness. In *Griffith v. Brymer*[3] the contract was concluded *after* the decision to cancel the procession on the expected date had been taken. The party who had hoped to view the procession was granted relief because of mistake. In *Krell v. Henry*,[4] the contract had been concluded before the cancellation, and the relief that was granted from its obligation is generally explained in terms of the frustration of its essential purpose.

The class of situation in which relief is granted for postcontractual surprises is further subdivided. In addition to cases of frustration like *Krell v. Henry*, where it is quite feasible to go through with the deal but there is little point in doing so, there are the cases falling under the rubric of impossibility or impracticability. The paradigm is *Taylor v. Caldwell*:[5] A music hall burned down; the owner sought release from his contractual obligation to performers who had engaged to use it on a particular day, on the ground that making the hall available was either a literal impossibility (if the contract meant a particular music hall) or a virtual impossibility (if the contract was to be viewed as requiring the licensor to reconstruct the music hall from the ground up). Though relief is granted in all these cases, confusion begins in the dichotomizing and subdichotimizing. I agree with critics of classical doctrine like Grant Gilmore,[6] who see here but a single problem. In *Griffith* as much as in *Krell* the parties did not expect the king's illness, and so in a sense they were equally mistaken in both. *Taylor* cannot, however, as easily be described as a case of mistake: It is not as if the parties mistakenly thought (as happened with the *Titanic*) that the hall was indestructible; rather they simply had not considered the matter at all.

It is not the presence of risk or uncertainty that vitiates agreement, since contracts generally are a device for allocating risks. In a contract for future delivery the seller takes on himself the risk that the goods will rise in price or that for some other reason it will become more burdensome for him to perform, and the buyer assumes reciprocal risks. The language of mistake suggests that certainty is the paradigm, but in fact contracts are largely a deliberate attempt to deal with uncertainty. The parties might have allocated the risk of the king's illness or of the fire, but they had not done so. And parties may allocate risks as to existing as well as to future circumstances. The prospector who buys a claim is taking a risk about the presence of minerals. In the celebrated case of *Wood v. Boynton*[7] the court upheld the sale for one dollar of an unidentified stone, which turned out to be a rough diamond, as involving in effect a gamble on the part of the buyer and seller as to the stone's value; while in *Sherwood v. Walker*[8] the court found that the seller had not transferred nor had the buyer paid for the chance that an apparently barren prize cow was in fact pregnant.

That the presence of risk, which is common to these cases, is not the cause of the difficulty is illustrated by yet another celebrated case, *Raffles v. Wichelhaus*,[9] in which a buyer refused to accept delivery of a shipment of cotton arriving in Liverpool from Bombay on the ship *Peerless*, as he had contracted to do, because the *Peerless* he had had in mind had sailed in October, while the seller's ship *Peerless* had sailed in December.* To speak of problems of risk, allocated or unallocated, in that case seems not a little strained. The straightforward point is that the two parties, though they seemed to have agreed, had not agreed in fact. And this—not mistake or risk—is at the heart of all of these cases: There just is no agreement as to what is or turns out to be an important aspect of the arrangement.[10] In *Raffles* there was agreement to purchase cotton from India shipped on a ship named *Peerless*. As it turned out, there was no

---

*Since the contract had been concluded, the Union had captured the important cotton port of New Orleans, which it had previously blockaded, and the price of cotton was declining steeply. (This point is made by Gilmore, supra note 1, at 37 n.87.) The court treated contracts for cotton from the two ships as if they were as different as contracts to star two actors both of whom coincidentally had the same name.

agreement at all on the crucial issue of which ship *Peerless*. Similarly in the coronation cases and *Taylor* there was agreement about some things, but none about risks (the king's illness, fire) that might have been covered and that turned out to be crucial. So risk comes into it, but only as one element about which the parties might have reached agreement but unfortunately did not. In all of these cases the court is forced to sort out the difficulties that result when parties think they have agreed but actually have not. The one basis on which these cases cannot be resolved is on the basis of the agreement — that is, of contract as promise. The court cannot enforce the will of the parties because there are no concordant wills. Judgment must therefore be based on principles external to the will of the parties.

It is not surprising that classical contract law was uncomfortable with these cases. They made nonvoluntary principles of obligation potentially applicable to every contract. Disappointed parties will have a great incentive to describe circumstances in ways that escape the explicit terms of their contracts. Matters can always be raised that genuinely were not the subject of the agreement, so that the court cannot avoid the question (not covered in the agreement itself) of how crucial these unprovided matters are: What if it had rained so that the coronation procession went faster and the view from the windows was partially obscured by spectators' umbrellas, or what if there had been only one ship *Peerless* but the parties had misspelled the name?

In the face of such pressures classical contract law sought refuge in a number of doctrinal devices, which made it look as if the cases were being determined by the will of the parties and nothing else after all. One such device is the reference to presumed intent.[11] It is a truism in the philosophy of language that in interpreting a person's words we are not guessing at the hidden but determined content of some list of meanings in the speaker's head.[12] Rather our concerns particularize, render concrete, inchoate meanings. (So when a person refers to all the even numbers between 10 and 1000, he intends to refer also to the number 946, though that number may not figure explicitly on some list in his head.) Yet at some point it becomes necessary to say not that this is what the speaker meant but rather that this is what the speaker might have meant had he thought of it. Similarly in contract law there is a vaguely marked boundary between interpreting what was agreed to and interpolating terms to which the parties in all probability would have agreed but did not.

The further courts are from the boundary between interpretation and interpolation, the further they are from the moral basis of the promise principle and the more palpably are they imposing an agreement. That this is a term the parties might have agreed to is just one kind of reason courts may have for imposing a term on them to which they have not in fact agreed. That decision is the courts' and not the parties', as is shown by the fact that there are some terms courts would not impose even if they believed the parties might have agreed to them had they thought about them. Courts would, for instance, insist that the terms they impose be fair, that they take the interests of both parties into account — even if perhaps the parties themselves might have been less fastidious. So as we move further from actual intention the standard of presumed intention tends to merge into the other substantive standards used to solve the problems caused by a failure in the agreement.[13]

Another of the classical law's evasions of the inevitability of using noncontractual·principles to resolve failures of agreement is recourse to the so-called objective standard of interpretation.[14] In the face of a claim of divergent intentions, the court imagines that it is respecting the will of the parties by asking what somebody else, say the ordinary person, would have intended by such words of agreement. This may be a reasonable resolution in some situations, but it palpably involves imposing an external standard on the parties. Both the reasonableness of this approach and its origin in nonpromissory standards of justice are clearest in cases of what is called unilateral mistake.[15] In such cases only one of the parties is surprised by what happens or by what is revealed to have been the case all along.

I. Seller, a dealer in old musical instruments, making no representations sells to buyer a pleasant but unremarkable early nineteenth century violin for eight hundred dollars — a customary price. Buyer, however, firmly believes that he has stumbled upon a Guarnerius worth at least twenty times the purchase price. On later receiving conclusive proof that he is wrong, buyer seeks relief from his bargain.[16]

II. Employee, fearing a recession in his field of endeavor, concludes a two-year contract of employment with employer, at a somewhat lower wage than would be paid in a contract terminable at will. Six months later employer's business suffers a decline in orders, and he seeks to discharge employee on the grounds that he had not expected this turn of events and that he should therefore be released from his obligations.

It will come as no surprise that courts would not entertain the claim of mistake in the first case or of frustration or impracticability in the second. Yet if we believe buyer and employer they, just as much as the seller of the supposedly barren cow in *Sherwood* or the hopeful spectator in *Krell*, have been saddled with risks they had not agreed to assume. They may deserve what they get, but not because it is a risk they have chosen to run. To get around the fact that this deserving is not based on their consent, courts have proposed an analysis that (*a*) there was an agreement to something (the sale of *this* violin, *these* terms of employment), and (*b*) the further mistaken assumptions not being shared, but being unilateral only, do not vitiate the force of that agreement. As cases like *Sherwood* and *Griffith* show, the fact that there was agreement on something is hardly enough to conclude the issue.\* Nor is the area of disagreement negligible in the two hypotheticals. The law emphasizes the point that the erroneous assumption is not shared, but this hardly makes a consensus where because of divergent assumptions on a crucial matter there is none. The contract is enforced in these cases of unilateral mistake in spite of this lack of agreement and, therefore, on other than promissory principles. The most likely principle acknowledges that one party in each case is being forced to bear a loss he had not knowingly assumed, but that the other party supposed that the risk of this loss had been allocated between them, and so that as between the two parties the one who had acted reasonably and in the ordinary course should not have his expectations disappointed. He should not be disappointed because (1) if a loss is inevitable and both parties are innocent, the careless man should not be able to cast that loss on the prudent, and (2) the chances that buyer's or employer's reservations are an afterthought are too great to warrant a systematic legal inquiry.[17]

The first of these reasons may be referred to consideration of fairness or to the encouragement of due care. The second reason is con-

---

\*All kinds of remarkable logic is chopped regarding whether the agreement is about the substance or a mere quality, the thing itself or an accident. See Francis de Zulueta, *The Roman Law of Sale: Introduction and Select Texts* 28-30 (Oxford, 1945). Thus, for instance, in *Wood* the agreement was held to be about the thing itself—this stone—while in *Sherwood* it was concluded that a barren cow and a pregnant one are somehow essentially different things. Of course all this is nonsense. Some measure of nonconsensus is inevitable, and how much will vitiate the deal is a matter of degree.

cerned not with the ultimate equities but with problems of administration. Both these considerations rely on grounds distinct from the promissory principle. This is shown in variations on unilateral mistake cases, where the nonmistaken party knew of the other's misconceptions (for example, seller knew buyer thought he was getting a Guarnerius), or even where he had reason to know,[18] or where — as some cases have suggested — though he did not know, the loss suffered by the mistaken party would be very great and the non-mistaken party would not lose any fair opportunity if the deal were undone.[19] The courts do not entertain such considerations in order to enforce what the parties agreed, since they did not agree at all in the premises. As the parties cannot agree, the court can only look to extrinsic standards of fairness for a solution. The futile attempt to bring these cases under the promise principle only plays into the hands of those who see nonpromissory principles of fairness at work throughout the law of contract.*

The law is more easily moved to intervene (1) where both parties make either the same or complementary mistakes (that is, cases of mutual mistake as in *Raffles*), or (2) where risks eventuate to which neither party had attended. Some resolution is necessary. The cases of relief for mutual mistake appear to pose a more serious challenge to the conception of contract as promise, for the law imposes an outcome (usually no more than an undoing of the transaction) that is based on the will of neither party. In the cases of unilateral mistake the will of at least *one* of the parties is effectuated — so we do not have so naked an example of imposition *ab extra*. Similarly, in those cases of impossibility and frustration where relief is granted we have the same appearance of imposing a result previously decreed by neither party. These cases, however, are also compatible with the conception that mutually self-imposed promissory obligation (the will of the parties) is the very life of contract. For one may ask what it would even mean to give effect to "the will of the parties" in a case where the parties had no convergent will on the matter at hand.

---

*Contracts by incompetent persons provide another illustration of the same range of problems. It seems correct to say, as the older cases did, that an insane person should not be taken to have expressed his will in a legally binding way. But it does not follow that therefore one who innocently dealt with such a person and cannot be restored to his former situation should bear the burden of that disability — remaining unpaid, for instance, for goods the insane person bought and cannot return. See generally Richard Danzig, *The Capability Problem in Contract Law* (Mineola, N.Y., 1978).

## LETTING THE LOSS LIE WHERE IT FALLS

One response of classical theory has been to deny any title to relief in such cases, insisting instead on a "strict," "literal" construction of the contract, come what may. Gilmore gives *Stees v. Leonard* as an example of this Draconian attitude.[20] A contractor, encountering unexpectedly swampy terrain, almost completes a promised structure, but it collapses. He rebuilds. It collapses again. Finally, he throws up his hands. Williston and other hard-liners have it that the builder is not excused from his promised performance.[21] (In the actual case, the owner sued primarily for a return of progress payments.) Since the contractor's bond obligates him to build, he must build, build and build again. This harsh, silly result is a stock example for critics of just where the liberal, or will, or promissory theory leads. Such harsh results are unacceptable, but the theory of contract as promise does not require them. Indeed *no* coherent theory can require such a conclusion. By demonstrating the incoherence of this so-called strict view, I show that no merely harsh theory could entail it.

The strict or literal view always enforces or ratifies *some* distribution of risk. In *Stees v. Leonard* the court allocated the risk of collapse to the builder. If no relief is granted to licensees of rooms along the route of the canceled coronation procession, the risk of cancellation is by implication imposed on them and not on those who hire out these rooms. Now why is that allocation of risks more "strict" than its opposite? Is it really because the contract says "to build a house" or "to rent rooms on . . ."? Is it because to release the builder or hirer implies a term such as "unless the ground is altogether softer than either of us considers reasonably likely" or "unless there is no procession to view"? But if this is the point why not argue the contrary; that there *should* be relief since the contract does not say "to build a house, whatever the condition of the ground," or "to hire the rooms on the date presently scheduled for the coronation, whether or not the coronation is subsequently canceled"? It is true that the actual words used admit of either interpretation, but why does that make the "harsher" interpretation the more eligible of the two possibilities? I suspect because of a lingering prejudice that the harsher interpretation is the simpler, the more unqualified, the more natural interpretation, while that which allows an excuse requires the court to add language, to superimpose something on the will of the parties. But it is just the point that on the issues in question the parties *had no will at all,* so that any resolution of the problem is necessarily imposed by the court. In short there has just been an accident, and any resolution of the accident is a kind of judgment, a kind of intervention.[22]

I suspect that the strict or literal view is related to the belief that accident losses in general should lie where they fall. The usual domain for letting the loss lie where it falls is the law of torts, and commentators have noted that the attitude that gave rise to the strict view in contracts displayed itself as well in an aversion to shifting losses in the law of torts. As Gilmore puts it, on this view ideally nobody was ever liable for anything.[23] But what does it mean to say even in tort law that the loss lies where it falls? It is worth clarifying this, since it is my contention that mistake and impossibility are a species of accident too—contractual accident.

The intuitive idea is that the burden of an accident should remain with whoever happens to have been hurt. Now, the injured party may decide to take the matter into his own hands and shift the loss to someone else (the injurer or a third party) so that thereafter the loss lies *there.* If a thief steals, unless the law helps the victim or the victim helps herself, the loss will lie with the victim. If an assailant punches you in the nose, the loss absent redress lies with you. Thus letting the loss lie where it falls does not describe an order at all, since nothing intrinsically tells us where this nonlegal imposition of burdens should stop. After all, why should it stop after the first link in the chain of events, why should not the victim at the end of the first link pass it on to someone else and then to someone else? This point is vital in the domain of contracts. For if losses were truly to be allowed to lie where they fall, then no contract would ever be enforced. If somebody ended up losing because he trusted in the promise of another, why the more fool he! Contract law enforces promises and does not allow a disappointed party to bear his disappointment simply because it has fallen upon him, any more than the law of torts allows the victim of an assault or of a reckless act to bear the costs that another would force on him. Some losses, on the other hand, are allowed to lie where they fall: If I trip and fall while walking along the beach, or if my business is ruined by a more efficient competitor, or if I make an unlucky specualtion in the currency markets. The reasons why some losses are shifted and others not are as various as the law itself, but there must *be* reasons. Letting the loss lie where it falls is not an argument, a reason; at best it restates one possible conclusion of an argument.

There are several general attitudes behind the inclination to let losses lie where they fall. One such attitude shrinks from the intervention that shifting losses entails, but this is only an attitude, not a theory, since as we have seen it cannot be systematically adhered to. At most it expresses a preference for nonintervention other things being equal, but then we need a theory of when things are indeed equal. A related attitude sees in loss shifting a threat to individual autonomy, since forcing others to share losses correspondingly threatens the chances of enjoying the gains from individual talents, efforts, and accomplishments. Yet this too is only a vague attitude until it is fleshed out by a theory of responsibility and of rights, a theory that identifies when a particular individual is responsible for his own or another's good or ill fortune and when an act is an exercise of one's own or a violation of another's rights. Finally, the confused attitude of social Darwinism, which once enjoyed a certain currency,* may have suggested that refusing to shift losses would allow the stronger to triumph over the less fit and the race—or whatever—to improve.[24] Since this last posture would make all law and all morality irrelevant, we need consider it no further.

This same set of confused attitudes lurks behind the notion that if an agreement is expressed in general words, and if those general words appear to cover a surprising specific case, then the burden of this surprise should lie where it will fall as a result of taking those general words as covering that specific case, even when neither party meant them to. To the extent that this notion has any appeal at all, it is as a rather confused and approximate statement of another, more coherent conception—a conception that, however, will often lead to quite different results. Now why should we take those words to include the unintended, surprising, specific result? The general words might *usually* imply this specific result. But in the instance of *this* contract and *these* parties, by hypothesis neither party meant or foresaw that these general words should cover this specific case. Perhaps a promisor should not be allowed to claim that she did not mean by a term what is generally implied by that term. But if she is not allowed to excuse herself by showing this private,

*Holmes, whom Gilmore associates with a predilection for letting losses lie where they fall, was more than a little drawn to this attitude. See Gilmore, supra note 1, at 14-17; Mark Howe, *Justice Oliver Wendell Holmes* II, 44-49 (Cambridge, 1963).

special intention, it is not because we doubt that sometimes people truly have such special intentions. Rather we may bar such a claim as a matter of fairness to the other party or as a matter of practical convenience. We rather suspect either (1) that the claimant did mean what is usually meant, took her chances, and is now trying to get out of what has turned into a bad deal; or (2) that though *she* didn't mean it, her opposite number did, and reasonably assumed that *she* did mean it, so that it would be unfair to disappoint the opposite party's expectations now by urging some surprising, unexpected, secret intention. But this is not turning your back and allowing the loss to lie where it falls. These are perfectly reasonable, practical grounds for administering a system that in general seeks to effectuate the true intentions of the parties. Where we really can be confident that neither party intended to cover this particular case, and where we can reach that conclusion without fearing a spreading disintegration of confidence in contractual obligations generally, no reason remains for enforcing this contract.

## PARALLELS WITH GENERAL LEGAL THEORY: AN EXCURSION

One possible source of the "strict" view of mistake and impossibility is a (mistaken) analogy to the proposition that there are no gaps in the law. This proposition, which is part of most conceptions of a mature legal system, holds that the legal system covers every question that might be brought up within it. There is no action on which the law cannot deliver judgment, decreeing the action to be either permitted, forbidden, or required. The judgment of "non-liquet" is in principle excluded.[25] Ronald Dworkin has shown how this axiom of completeness is an embarrassment for one particular kind of legal theory, legal positivism, and more particularly that variety of positivism made known by John Austin under the heading of the "command" theory,[26] the theory that conceptualizes all law as the "will" or "command" of a sovereign. In every genuinely novel case, one as to which no one has spoken before, the will theory of law confronts a dilemma. Dworkin gives this example: The legislature has said that sacrilegious contracts are invalid. Is a contract signed on Sunday invalid? The legislation is silent on this point. Putting together this positivist axiom that the law is what the sovereign (the legislature) says it is and the axiom of completeness, it appears that since the legislature has *not* created a right to enforce the contract, there is no such right. But if it also has not said that the contract is invalid, then there is a right to have it enforced. One positivist gambit to save the will theory of law from this contradiction proposes the judge as a kind of subsidiary sovereign, issuing commands and thus *creating* legal rights in the gaps left by the commands of the principal sovereign. But this will not do; lawyers and litigants do not assume that in "hard" or controversial cases they have no rights until the judge announces his decision. Rather they argue to the judge to grant them a right that they claim they already have. They appeal to principles that they take to be binding on the judge, and expect from him not an act of legislation or of will, but an act of reason, an argument and conclusion based on principles of law. But if this is correct, then what the law is depends not on the identification of some previous act of will of some sovereign, but on the reasoned elaboration of principles—including moral principles—which are now seen to be as much a part of the law as are legislative decrees. And of course this intimate interpenetration of law and morals is just what Dworkin argued for and the positivist will theory of law seeks to deny.[27]

There are important points of contact (beyond just the name) between the will theory of law and the will theory of contracts. The same legal theorists who propounded the will theory of law as a way to make law determinate and distinct from controversial issues of morality were attracted to the will theory of contracts as a way of making persons' rights and duties as far as possible a function of their own will and not of standards of justice external to that will. The two theories have shared some of the same critics as well. Since the will theory comes a cropper as a general theory of law, these critics suppose that it must also fail as a theory of contract law: If law is not just the will of the sovereign but is in part a moral phenomenon, neither may contract be based on the will of the parties. Thus the will theory of contract is thought to be refuted by analogy. Those seeking to refute the will theory of contract brandish mistake and impossibility in the same way that those who seek to refute the will theory of law brandish the novel or "hard" cases. And those who would defend the will theory either in contracts or in general legal theory are tempted to the same dubious move in both instances: They hide in the nonexistent refuge of general words and strict construction. In both cases, they attempt to show that somehow what the legislature has said, or what the words of the contract provide, in itself allows a principled determination of the embarrassing case. But I hope I have said enough to show that that way lies only paradox.

Though the embarrassment of the unprovided-for case is fatal to the will theory of law, it is not at all fatal to a will theory of contracts properly conceived, for there is no equivalent in the doctrine of contracts to the axiom that the law has no gaps. The law must have an answer for all disputes raised before it. There is, however, no equivalent necessity that a contract have a determinative answer to all disputes that might arise relating to the contract's subject matter. Though it is fatal to a theory of law that law have gaps—and thus the will theory of law is refuted—it is not fatal to a will theory of contracts that contractual arrangements have gaps. After all, the law itself imposes contractual liability on the basis of a complex of moral, political, and social judgments. The limits of that liability must depend on judgments; what is on the other side (the noncontractual side) of those limits is also within the control of those judgments which make up the law. And so gaps in a contract pose no theoretical problem whatever. Gaps are a problem when we do not know how to fill them, but we know perfectly well how to fill the gaps in a contract. There is no bare flesh showing, as it were, when relations between persons are not covered by contractual clothing. These relations take place under the general mantle of the law. Indeed, the very absence of gaps in the law makes it easy to admit that there may be gaps in contract. For when relations between parties are not governed by the actual promises they have made, they are governed by residual general principles of law.

## FILLING THE GAPS

It would be irrational to ignore the gaps in contracts, to refuse to fill them. It would be irrational not to recognize contractual accidents and to refuse to make adjustments when they occur. The gaps cannot be filled, the adjustments cannot be governed, by the promise principle. We have already encountered the two competing residuary principles of civil obligation that take over when promise gives out: the tort principle to compensate for harm done, and the restitution principle for benefits conferred. Each of these has some application, but only a limited or puzzling one, to the cases that concern us. If a contracting party has knowingly concealed or negligently overlooked an eventuality that sharply alters the risks — for example, if the owner in the *Stees* case knew or easily could have learned of the difficult condition of his land — we may force him to bear the resulting loss for that reason. If a party has conferred benefits (built something, paid in advance) under a contract that subsequently fails because of frustration, the benefit should be paid for or returned. In the cases arising out of the cancellation of the coronation, for instance, the rooms overlooking the procession route were valuable just for that purpose and could be rented again when the coronation was rescheduled. To allow the owners to collect twice would have been preposterous. (But what if there had been no later procession?)

Unfortunately in many cases both parties are harmed, neither is at fault, neither benefits. The half-built house is destroyed by an earthquake.[28] The half-built machine is rendered useless by a government regulation.[29] The program printed for the canceled yacht race is of no interest to anyone.[30] In such situations a distinct third principle for apportioning loss and gain comes into play: the principle of sharing.[31] Consider these cases:

III. A man and a women spending the night together in an inn discover an envelope containing a large sum of money at the back of a bureau drawer. The original owner cannot be traced. Should the owner of the inn, the man, or the women, keep the money, or should they share it?[32]

IV. In an unusually severe storm a freighter loses some but not all of the valuable cargo of several shippers. Should the loss lie where it falls, should it be borne by the owner of the vessel, or should it be shared among all the shippers and the owner of the vessel?[33]

These cases point up the difference between sharing on one hand and the benefit and harm principles on the other. In benefit and harm the predicate for shifting a burden or an advantage is the responsible act of one of the parties. Such responsibility may arise out of culpability — including negligence — a voluntary act, or a prior assumption of responsibility, as by a contract. As cases III and IV illustrate, however, in some situations there may be no basis for holding the parties responsible or accountable to one another. Rather, persons in some relation, perhaps engaged in some common enterprise, suffer an unexpected loss or receive an unexpected gain. The sharing principle comes into play where no agreement obtains, no one in the relationship is at fault, and no one has conferred a benefit. Sharing applies where there are no rights to respect. It is the principle that would apply if a group of us were to land together on some new planet.[34] It is peculiarly appropriate to filling the gaps in agreements, to picking up after contractual accidents. Applied to the collapsing house in *Stees* or the half-built machine now rendered useless, it says that the loss would not lie where it falls, but the parties would share that loss—which would mean perhaps that the owner or buyer would pay for half of the useless work that was done. And this is the direction in which courts are now moving.[35]

Why, you might ask, should just the parties to the agreement share the benefits and burdens? In the case of the half-built machine why should not the government pay part of the cost? In the case of the house, why should not the neighbors chip in, since the earthquake damage might have happened to them? In the case of the money found in the inn, why should not the boon be spread more widely? The question necessarily leads into very general issues of political philosophy, and the hesitation to recognize and to fill gaps in contractual arrangements may have arisen as a result of worries at this most general level. Admitting a general obligation to share is rightly seen as a threat to the principles of autonomy and personal responsibility. If we must share the benefits and burdens of random contractual accidents, why not share all of life's benefits and burdens? Why not view good and bad luck in investments, choice of occupation, or market strategy as accidents to be evened out by sharing? And indeed why not view even variation in talents, character, or disposition as accidents? In the end there would be full sharing, and no one would enjoy the benefits or bear the responsibilities of his personal choices—indeed of his person.[36] In such a system the concept of autonomy, which lies behind contract as promise, would be rendered meaningless.

Modern liberal democracies and liberal political theory have sought to develop a concept of sharing that yet leaves the person and his liberties intact. As I argue in greater detail in chapter 7, the accommodation is sought through the basic division of function in the modern welfare state between private market (contractual) autonomy and general redistributive welfare schemes. This accommodation assumes that the obligation to share is a general one in

71

which all should participate by tax contributions. The system attempts to reduce the extreme disparities in overall wealth that undermine the possibility of community and at the same time to provide both fair opportunities for advancement and a guaranteed social minimum. Such a system is designed to provide a framework, a structure within which individuals may indeed exercise their autonomy and reap the benefits or suffer the consequences of their choices. Though the exact formula for what constitutes tolerable disparities and a decent social minimum must be subject to shifting, political judgments, I affirm that this structure and its purposes are in principle sound.

Does this mean that there is no room for the principle of sharing in the contractual domain, that its admission there would threaten to undermine the healthy compromise of autonomy and community implicit in liberal democracies? I think not. By engaging in a contractual relation A and B become no longer strangers to each other. They stand closer than those who are merely members of the same political community. Like the persons in my examples they are joined in a common enterprise, and therefore they have some obligation to share unexpected benefits and losses in the case of an accident in the course of that enterprise. Just as we do not say that C must come in to share those losses, so we do not say that A and B must share losses that are wholly outside the scope of their enterprise.

This appealing resolution has problems. Is not the contractual enterprise just that enterprise in which mutual obligations have been willingly undertaken; and yet do not contractual accidents occur precisely because no mutual engagements have been made; so that we are constructing a kind of nonconsensual penumbra around the consensual core? In terms of what do we construct this penumbra? Not in terms of the wills or promises of the parties. Obviously some standard of sharing *external* to the intention of the parties must control. But if the law is free to impose standards external to the intention of contractual parties to the end of fairly dividing up losses in the case of a contractual accident, does this not show that principles of sharing are available potentially to allocate burdens and benefits among any set of citizens at all? If so, then not only is the contractual nexus unnecessary to create the focusing predicate *for* sharing, sharing itself may be seen as so powerful a principle as to overwhelm that nexus, reversing the effects of agreements even where there has been no accident.

We need not go this far. Those in concrete or personal relations must have a greater care for each other than those who stand to each other in the abstract relation of fellow citizens, or fellow man.[37] By this principle family members and friends are owed and may engross a greater measure of our concern than abstract justice prescribes. By this principle too, direct or intentional harm constitutes a wrong. Making another person the object of your intention, a step along the way in your plans, particularizes that person and forms a concrete relation between you and him. Typically such concrete relations are freely chosen. Though some family ties are not chosen, ties of friendship are, and, as to harm, the intention to harm a specified other person (stranger or not) is quintessentially voluntary.

A contractual relation is a good example of a concrete relation that may give rise to a more focused duty to share another's good or ill fortune. The relation is, after all, freely chosen. Indeed this is the same idea as that the contractual parties are in a common enterprise – an enterprise they chose to enter.[38] True, the bond does extend beyond the explicit terms of the contract, since the problems we are concerned with are by hypothesis not explicitly disposed of in the contract. The contract does, however, also imply a limit to the obligation. If I have furnished machinery to your factory over the years I am to some unspecified further degree involved in your manufacturing endeavor, but surely not in the misfortunes that befall you in some unrelated speculation, or in your family travails. If I have agreed to sell you a small standard part, an extension cord or a light bulb, my implication in your venture (and yours in mine) will have very little penumbra beyond the actual agreement of sale. Thus in filling the gaps it is natural to look to the agreement itself for some sense of the nature and extent of the common enterprise. Since actual intent is (by hypothesis) missing, a court respects the autonomy of the parties so far as possible by construing an allocation of burdens and benefits that reasonable persons would have made in this kind of arrangement. (It treats the contract as a kind of charter or constitution for the parties' relation.) This is, as I argued earlier, an inquiry with unavoidably normative elements: "Reasonable" parties do not merely seek to accomplish rational objectives; they do so constrained by norms of fairness and honesty. Finally, this recourse to principles of sharing to fill the gaps does not threaten to overwhelm the promissory principle, for the simple reason that the parties are quite free to control the meaning and extent of their relation by the contract itself.

# 6

# GOOD FAITH

**T**he most direct challenge to
the conception of contract law as a coherent expression of the principle of autonomy is thought to come from the doctrines of good faith,
unconscionability, and duress.[1] These doctrines explicitly authorize
courts in the name of fairness to revise contractual arrangements or
to overturn them altogether. Good faith is a way of dealing with a
contractual party: honestly, decently. It is an adverbial notion suggesting the avoidance of chicanery and sharp practice (bad faith)
whether in coming to an agreement or in carrying out its terms.
Duress is a vice inhering in the pressure used to procure the agreement, while unconscionability refers to a vice in the agreement itself:
An unconscionable agreement is unfairly one-sided; it takes advantage of the weakness of one of the parties. (Although an agreement

procured by duress is also likely to be one-sided, it need not be, so the two doctrines may diverge.)

These doctrines are said to challenge the concept of contract as promise because in one way or another they deny that promise is sufficient to define the relations between contracting parties. Duties assumed under the contract may not be enforced if the agreement is judged to be unconscionable or to have been procured by duress; duties not explicitly assumed by the parties may be imposed if required by good faith. Since the application of these doctrines depends on a court's judgment of fairness, it seems as if contractual relations depend not on the will of the parties but on externally imposed substantive moral judgments of what the relations between the parties should be. That there are rights and duties that have not been voluntarily assumed and agreed upon can of itself hardly present a challenge, for few indeed suggest that all rights and duties, all relations between citizens, are based on explicit agreement — see, for instance, chapters 5's discussion of the court's duty to fill gaps in an agreement by use of legal and moral principles of fairness. The challenge rather is this: that even where there has been an explicit agreement, it is not the agreement but judgments of fairness and the substantive good that define how people should behave toward each other. Admitting force or fraud as an invalidating circumstance is said to show that contract does not have its basis in the promise principle, in the principle of giving effect to obligations freely assumed by the contracting parties. Rather, contract is shown to be what all law inevitably must be: the imposition *ab extra* of a decision designed to achieve what courts and society judge to be a fair distribution of burdens and advantages. After all, it is argued, greater strength and facility in deception are just two advantages among many that may cause the balance of a bargain to tip in favor of one who is better endowed. Once we admit that bargains may be overturned or revised because of an imbalance in advantages of this sort, the way lies open to review and revise agreements generally in terms of their fairness. Indeed at the end of this road lies the revision of an agreement just because of the balance of advantage *in its outcome* without reference at all to some prior imbalance in the situation of the parties. If there had been no preexisting imbalance, why, after all, would an imbalanced agreement have ensued? Unfair results are treated as conclusive evidence of unfair procedures, and the two kinds of judgments are thought to merge.[2]

In my discussion of fraud in connection with good faith and of threats in connection with duress I show that this is a specious argument, that there are grounds for condemning fraud and force that do not at all refer to the balance of advantage that results from their use. Indeed it is a nonsequitur to argue that because the use of force and fraud may confer advantages in bargaining, therefore the general purpose behind condemning them is to achieve some desired balance of advantages between contracting parties (or indeed between all citizens). In short, although condemning bargains reached by force or fraud will have distributive effects, it does not follow that redistributive aims lie behind these judgments. To make my affirmative case, however, I must offer a theory that explains the doctrines of fraud and duress and yet leaves the conception of contract as promise intact.

A subtler attack on contract as promise builds primarily on the concept of good faith. This attack affirms the relational basis of contract law, but locates it elsewhere than in the deliberate assumption by promisors of a set of limited rights and duties. On this view, contractual relations establish ties of community between the parties, and such ties generate their own moral imperatives, quite apart from the limited obligations the parties may have assumed in creating the relation. This view is (and is intended to be) a deliberate rejection and reversal of Henry Sumner Maine's classic thesis in *Ancient Law* that modern law has moved away from status relations to relations founded on promise, that is, relations defined by the will of the parties. In contrast to the redistributive thesis, this view does not hold that a set of obligations is imposed on the parties by society for general social purposes; but rather, the relationship itself is seen as implying moral duties and constraints. Many have sounded this retreat from Maine's conception—Macneil, Fuller, Gilmore, Kessler, Atiyah.[3] In a recent, influential article Duncan Kennedy contrasts individualism to altruism and proposes altruism as the competing morality for contractual relations. Altruism is a morality of sharing and sacrifice. If, as a relation develops, one party comes to enjoy great gains, he must share these gains with his partner. If he suffers severe losses, his partner should sacrfice and assume some of the burden of those losses. Individualism, by contrast, allows each party to retain whatever advantages he enjoys and gives him no claim to relief in distress. The parties' duties to each other are just those they have assumed and no more.[4] The model of the altruistic relation is the family, contrasted to the harsh individualism of commercial relations. On the view of Fuller, Macneil, and Kennedy, however, the dichotomy is false, and all relations—whether of friendship or of commerce—may be moved by the ethic of altruism, and if not so moved spontaneously, should be shaped to that ideal by the intervention of the courts. And since altruism is primarily interested in making adjustments as a relationship develops, there is naturally associated with it the rejection of individualism's concern to identify and enforce the original agreement according to its terms. This rejection takes the form of an attack on a vaguely defined vice called formalism. In the discussion of good faith I examine the charge that contract as promise is affected by this vice.[5]

These two attacks on contract as promise—the attack in the name of redistribution and that in the name of altruism—are related. Since altruism requires sharing, it too is an instance of pursuing redistributive goals through contract law. The two critiques are distinct, however, in focus. Altruism focuses on sharing within a particular relation. Thus it seems to be a less thoroughgoing attack, for at least it recognizes the special significance of the particular relations the parties themselves have established. In another sense, however, it is more subversive of individualism. Redistribution—as modern welfare economics teaches[6]—might at least rest content with defining broad endowments of wealth and resources, which the parties would then be free to trade as they wished (that is, by making individualistic contracts). Altruism denies individualism this contractual refuge. And of course nothing about altruism requires that it be confined to sharing and sacrifice between contractual partners or others in close relationships. Such special relationships might be claimed to impose *additional* duties of sharing and sacrifice.

## "HONESTY IN FACT"

The Uniform Commercial Code defines good faith as honesty in fact.[7] On the face of it honesty has nothing to do with sharing, with altruism, or with an active concern for one's fellow man. An honest man may drive a hard bargain, but does so openly, candidly. It might be said that honesty is the virtue most closely associated with classical individualism, and with the principle of autonomy:[8] If a person is well informed and in secure enjoyment of his rights, then whatever arrangements he chooses to make deserve to be honored. They represent a free man's rational decision about how to dispose of what is his, how to bind himself. The quintessence of honesty is the Victorian gentleman, who though rigid, perhaps ungenerous, a hard bargainer, keeps his word and does not lie. Honesty assures, first, that one will not mislead another as to the facts in order to profit by the other's misinformed decision. It assures also that engagements once made will be honored. Good faith as honesty may be viewed as a manifestation of the liberal belief in the objectivity of facts, in individual autonomy, and in the importance of keeping one's word.

Consider the leading case of *Obde v. Schlemeyer*.[9] The seller knew that his house was infested by termites, and knew also that he had done no more by way of treatment than to cover up and repair all visible signs of that infestation. The buyer had not, however, asked about termites, nor had the seller given any assurances about the condition of his house. Nevertheless a court held that the buyer had been defrauded and awarded him damages for the losses he had suffered.

What are we to say of this case? The seller certainly acted dishonestly, and if Schlemeyer had told an outright lie neither lawyer nor moralist would have the least difficulty with the case.[10] Lying is wrong, and thus it is an inadmissible way of procuring an advantage. I have argued this point at length elsewhere.[11] Here I relate the wrongness of lying to my thesis about the moral basis of promise and to the specious argument that the contractual prohibition of fraud is a form of redistribution.[12] In the vision I have been putting forward, the capacity to form true and rational judgments and to act on them is the heart of moral personality and the basis of a person's claim to respect as a moral being. A liar seeks to accomplish his purpose by creating a false belief in his interlocutor, and so he may be said to do harm by touching the mind, as an assailant does harm by laying hands on his victim's body. Further, a liar procures this advantage by preying on the other person's trust, for it is only by invoking the expectation of truthfulness that the lie does its work. This vice is compounded when the lie does its work in the context of a promise. A simple lie does harm because it is believed; a lie that is believed and so elicits the victim's promise does harm only if that promise is enforced. But to enforce the promise is to invoke *against the victim* the very morality of respect and trust that the liar betrayed in eliciting the promise. It is just possible to describe this condemnation of fraud as a redistribution of advantages, but it is hardly illuminating, since the "advantage" is one procured by violation of a moral principle that is not concerned with distributional concerns as such at all.

So lying is an easy case, but did Schlemeyer lie? He appears to have done "no more" than fail to disclose information he knew would be very helpful to the buyer. One can lie otherwise than in words. Schlemeyer covered up (literally) the traces of termite infestation, knowing that this would create a wrong impression on the buyer and surely intending that it should. Is this a lie? The critics of the conception of contract as promise argue that the concept of fraud is unstable, that it cannot be limited to some analytically defined or intuitively clear domain of clearly wrongful conduct, that it inevitably implies a duty to share information, which in turn inevitably admits a duty to share advantages in general. The *Obde* case might be thought to be the first step down this slippery slope to a general duty of sharing.

Consider this case:

> I. An oil company has made extensive geological surveys seeking to identify possible oil and gas reserves. These surveys are extremely expensive. Having identified one promising site, the oil company (acting through a broker) buys a large tract of land from its prosperous farmer owner, revealing nothing about its survey, its purposes, or even its identity. The price paid is the going price for farmland of that quality in that region.[13]

Is the purchaser's conduct here different from the seller's in *Obde*? Should we hold the seller here to his promise to sell the land, as we would *not* hold the buyer in *Obde*? Would it be correct to say that the purchaser deceived the seller? Unlike Schlemeyer, the oil company studiously avoided deceiving the farmer. It did not send its agent around dressed in overalls and chewing on a straw. Its inquiries were placed through a broker known to be acting for an unidentified purchaser. Now as a general matter the prohibition on lying can hardly entail a general duty to remove all instances of ignorance and error that might swim within your reach; you do no greater wrong if you fail to remove a stranger's error than if you fail to go out of your way to relieve some other unfulfilled want of a random stranger. If in Columbus, Ohio, there is a child who would be made happier if presented with an ice cream cone, this makes no moral claim upon you; neither does that child's mother's misconception that today's fine weather will last, which misconception causes her to leave home without an umbrella. You did not cause the distress; you are not using it for your purposes — and so also you did not cause the ignorance. The distress and the ignorance of themselves make no generalized claim on all those who might possibly relieve them.[14] In hypothetical case I, however, the oil company is not simply failing to relieve distress, not simply failing officiously to remove ignorance, it is making that ignorance the means by which it achieves its ends, increases its profit.

This case is just on the moving edge of the law's developing frontal system, and some modern writers argue for giving the farmer relief.[15] On what grounds? There was no lie. If fraud is recognized here then it does indeed seem that we are simply evening out the (informational) advantages between the parties. To sharpen our intuitions, consider this case.

II. The facts are the same as in case I, except that the oil company is seeking to obtain exploration rights not from a farmer but from a large natural resources holding company. The oil company is a small, venturesome wildcat exploration company, which is willing to take great risks and to rely on controversial geological data. Once again neither party states what its expectations are or what its basis for acting might be. The oil company proposes a price to the natural resources company, which accepts, and the arrangement is concluded.

The intuitive response to this case is entirely different from the response to the *Obde* facts, and lacks any of the ambivalence one might feel about the case of the oil company and the farmer. Why is this? Surely it is not because here we have corporations on either side of the transaction or because we feel some sentimental attachment to the interests of farmers. Nor is the wealth of the parties by itself significant. After all, the farmer may have been a very wealthy farmer, with extensive land holdings. If one is inclined to make the naive party's wealth significant, it is on the tacit assumption that wealth brings knowledge, experience, opportunities, so that a wealthy farmer in the previous hypothetical might be left with his bargain because he had made a deliberate calculation not to spend some of his wealth to obtain the information purchased by the oil company—or perhaps he did not reserve any rights in the event of mineral discoveries just because he was eager to procure what seemed a good price.

The conflicting intuitions in these cases can, I believe, be referred to the basic conception of contract as promise. For the obligation of promise does not take hold where the promisor has not knowingly undertaken that obligation. As we saw in chapter 5, where the parties have not intended to undertake an allocation of risk or advantages, the mere fact that the general words of what they have undertaken appear to cover an unexpected case should not of itself bind them in that case. There has been a mistake. Case I and *Obde* are indeed cases of mistake, to the extent that the contract is defective at all. The mistake in each case is unilateral: The seller in *Obde* knew of the termites. The oil company in I was at least knowingly gambling on the chance of oil; the farmer-seller was not. (The seller in II may have been gambling.) As we have seen, unilateral mistake presents the weaker case for relief, especially where one party to the bargain is simply trying to enforce what he thought the bargain was. But *Obde* is not like that. Schlemeyer knew of Obde's misconception;[16] indeed he helped to create it. In every mistake case, it is my thesis, not promise but the competing equities must be used to resolve the inevitable dilemma caused by a contractual accident. Where one of the parties causes the accident, however (as in *Obde*), the equities quite clearly do not favor him. His dishonorable behavior does not prevent the contract from coming into being—it did not come into being in any event. It rather prevents the cheat from claiming on grounds of equity that he should get the same benefit as he would have enjoyed in a foursquare contract.

The oil company cases are more difficult to dispose of in this way. One who causes another's mistake forfeits any equitable claim to enforce an imperfect deal, but in case I the oil company at most knew (and sought to profit by) the farmer's mistake. Nevertheless if it is allowed to enforce the deal, the reason cannot be because there was complete agreement about the subject matter of the promise. There was not. Though there is no general (altruistic) duty to aid, to share, and thus no general duty to share information in order to remove another's harmful misconception,* this imperfect agreement should

---

*Imagine this case: I see you are about to build a hotel on a lot near my restaurant, greatly to my benefit. I have no duty to tell you that the land is swampy so that the foundation will cost you more than you may be expecting to pay.

not be enforced unless there is some equitable ground for enforcing it. The fact that the oil company knowingly seeks to take advantage of the farmer's ignorance hardly raises such an equity in its favor. And without some equity the deal just dies.

We do of course feel ambivalence about these duty-to-disclose cases, as case II shows. For we are little inclined there to deny the oil company the fruits of its bargain. And indeed the law would generally hold for the oil company even in a case just like I.[17] The recently drafted *Restatement (Second) of Contracts* provides (in section 161) that "a person's non-disclosure of a fact known to him is equivalent to an assertion that the fact does not exist only if . . . (b) he knows that disclosure of the fact would correct a mistake of the other party as to a basic assumption on which that party made the contract *and* if non-disclosure of the fact amounts to a failure to act in good faith and in accordance with reasonable standards of fair dealing . . . " (emphasis added). The comment to that provision states explicitly that "a buyer of property, for example, is not ordinarily expected to disclose circumstances that make the property more valuable than the seller supposes." Why not? What lurking equity favors making a bargain for the oil company, though (if my analysis is correct) no true agreement exists? In case II we see that both parties belong to a world in which it is understood that research into and calculations about qualities enhancing the value of real property are the responsibility of each party. Thus in a very general way these risks are part of the assumptions of the deal. Or alternatively, the equities favor the oil company because these general background understandings have led it to invest resources in acquiring the relevant knowledge and that investment would be largely engrossed by the seller (who took none of the investment risks) if disclosure were required. The case of the farmer is difficult just because he may not be in on this game at all, and so the oil company's equities do not foreclose him in the same way. And yet there are equities for the oil company in case I as well. If these are the general conventions on which it has proceeded, there is no way for it to deal differently with the unusual person who is not aware of these conventions. We cannot make an exception for the farmer without turning over the largest part of the gain to him, though he took none of the risk.

Perhaps this is what is behind the *Restatement's* harsh-sounding remark: "If the other is indolent, inexperienced or ignorant, or if his judgment is bad or he lacks access to adequate information his adversary [!] is not generally expected to compensate for these deficiencies." The judgment is too sweeping. I would say rather that where the better-informed party cannot compensate for the other's defects without depriving himself of an advantage on which he is conventionally entitled to count, his failure to disclose will not cause the equities to tilt against him.

Anthony Kronman has recently written that these arguments in terms of encouraging investment in information show that the results in such cases do and should just depend on a policy of efficiency and redistribution. The decisions favor the oil company because even the sellers will be better off in the long run under a rule that encourages such investments in knowledge. And in general, argues Kronman, what contracts are enforced is (or should be) always just a function of what will make the least advantaged party to the particular kind of transaction better off.*[18] But this misconceives the argument. The oil company wins not because we want to encourage its future investments but because it would be unfair to defeat its past reasonable expectations. To be sure, our determination to be fair even in the face of sentimental pressures to favor a weaker party (the farmer) will encourage investment—that is, rational planning for the future. But Kronman gets the arguments exactly the wrong way around. Indeed, if we played fair with the oil company only because (and only so far as) this led to greater economic productivity or improved the situation of the least advantaged party, then our playing fair on a particular occasion would not create confidence and so would not even procure these supposed general benefits. In general we can get the social, collective benefits of trust only if we are faithful for the sake of trust itself, not just for the sake of the resulting benefits.

Those who take an instrumental view of the duty to disclose—whether their goal be efficiency alone or efficiency allocated to the least favored party—are right to this extent: Many of the conventions that establish the background expectation, that establish (in the words of the *Restatement*) "reasonable standards of fair dealing" do tend to produce efficient results. And perhaps some

*Kronman's formulation, Rawlsian in inspiration, is still economic and instrumental in form. Another version in the economic mode would ask simply whether a rule of disclosure was more efficient. Kronman used this formulation himself in an earlier work, supra note 9.

of these conventions have been adopted or have evolved just because they do lead to efficiency. It would be fallacious, however, to conclude from this that efficiency (or in Kronman's version, efficiency plus redistribution) should determine the result *in a particular case*, rather than the considerations of fairness I have just proposed.

First, these conventions of disclosure also have other moving forces. The most striking example is the duty to disclose of a party who stands in a relation of trust to the promisee: for instance if one of the parties holds himself out to act in the interests of the other (say as lawyer, guardian, or agent). Nondisclosure in such cases violates the trust created by the terms of that fiduciary relationship.[19] But perhaps these fiduciary cases show that not only efficiency but also an altruistic policy favoring weaker or more dependent persons determines what general duties will or will not be enforced. This is the thesis of those like Kennedy and Macneil, who stress the relational aspect of contract doctrine. Second, whether the background conventions are motivated by economic or by altruistic-relational concerns, both perspectives tend to miss the crucial point that these conventions *precede* the particular (failed) contractual encounter. As conventions they define expectations, permit planning, and constrain the court's pursuit of either efficiency or altruism in the particular case. For if efficiency or altruism were our sole concern, there would be no a priori reason why they might not be better served if courts sometimes took it upon themselves to decide particular cases on an ad hoc basis, free of the constraints of preexisting convention.[20] But courts generally do not operate on such an ad hoc basis, and they rarely admit it if they do—which tells powerfully against theses such as Kronman's or Kennedy's.[21]

Efficiency, redistribution, and altruism are certainly among the law's many goals. By pursuing those goals according, but only according, to established conventions—including conventions established prospectively or gradually by courts—the collectivity acknowledges that individuals have rights and cannot just be sacrificed to collective goals. The recourse to prior conventions permits individuals to plan, to consider and pursue their own ends. And once they have made and embarked on plans against this background it would be unjust to change the rules in midcourse by requiring unexpected disclosures and sharing just in case the plans succeed. Changes should be prospective only. Indeed if courts did ignore established conventions in acting as agents of social policy, then the collectivity would itself be guilty of the same breach of trust, the same bad faith condemned in transactions between individuals. (In the next chapter I elaborate this point in respect to property rights in general.)

Finally, this faithfulness to the background understandings that elicit individual plans and effort is the heart of the attitude that critics of individualism have caricatured under the name of formalism. A court seeking to maintain trust between the collectivity and individuals must inquire into the background understandings (including those established by prior decisions) of a particular case. For those who have no patience with anything but forward-looking policies of social betterment, this inquiry will seem a vain, even foolish exercise—as would scrupulous adherence to one's promises.[22] To be sure, in hard cases this interpretive quest may sometimes be both arcane and controversial.[23] On this too I will have more to say in the discussion that follows.

## GOOD FAITH IN PERFORMANCE

The concept of good faith is regularly invoked not only to condemn deception and lack of candor at the time a bargain is concluded, but also to require a forthcoming attitude, to condemn chicanery and sharp practice in the carrying out of contractual obligations.[24] This has led some to argue that at least at this later stage good faith implies a duty to share, a duty of altruism.[25] Thus while good faith as honesty is quite compatible with the concept of contract as promise, since only obligations knowingly assumed are freely assumed, good faith as loyalty (to use a contrast proposed by Roberto Unger)[26] imposes duties that go beyond the promise principle. A contract is seen as creating a kind of status relationship, like a contract of marriage or, in some countries, of employment, and that relationship then assumes a life of its own. Three standard cases will lend some concreteness to the consideration of good faith in performance.

In *Patterson v. Meyerhofer*,[27] plaintiff, a prospective purchaser of a parcel of land, agreed that defendant should acquire the land for her and then resell it to her at a specified price. She then successfully bid against defendant at the auction at which the parcel was put up for sale, and sued for damages for nonperformance. The court denied the claim on the ground that implicit in her contract with defendant was an obligation not to take actions interfering with her contractual partner's performance. In contrast to *Patterson* is *Iron*

*Trade Products Co. v. Wilkoff*,[28] in which the plaintiff had contracted to buy a quantity of used iron rails from the defendant and
later entered the market to purchase a large quantity of these rails
on his own account, thereby causing the price to rise and the defendant to experience difficulties in making the necessary purchases.
The court held that the buyer's conduct was in no sense a violation of
the contract, that parties dealing in a commodity consider
themselves free to speculate on their own account, and that anybody
who has made a forward contract for sale understands that all
potential actors in the market—including the forward purchaser—may continue to speculate in the market.

In *Neofotistos v. Harvard Brewing Co.*,[29] a brewery was bound
by a long-term contract with a farmer to supply him with all the
spent grain from its brewing operation for his use as cattle feed. The
brewery experienced a period of declining demand and ultimately
shut down. The farmer brought suit, saying that the shutdown was
in breach of the obligation of good faith. At one time courts tended
to find this kind of contract—to supply all of a purchaser's needs, or
to accept all of a producer's output—too indefinite to be enforceable. After all, they reasoned, what the buyer's needs would be
or what the seller would produce was up to him, and so in binding
oneself to buy or sell by this measure a party was not binding himself
at all. (Since he had bound himself to nothing, his promise was "illusory" and could not stand as consideration for the opposite party's
promise.) Later it was recognized that at least in *exclusive* output or
supply contracts the promisor had indeed significantly restricted his
freedom of action.[30] Harvard Brewing, for instance, could cease to
supply spent grain only if it ceased operation, and presumably there
were other factors than just the market for spent grain influencing
its decisions of whether and how much to brew. The Uniform Com-
mericial Code has gone further, however, requiring that the decision to curtail output must be made in good faith, and suggesting
that doing so merely to avoid losses is not in good faith, while cur-
tailment to avoid bankruptcy is permissible.[31]

None of these cases compels the conclusion that good faith in performance undermines the autonomous nature of contractual obligation. In each case a reasonable interpretation of the parties' agreement, of their original intentions, against the background of normal
practices and understandings in that kind of transaction, would be
quite sufficient to provide a satisfactory resolution. In *Patterson*, for

instance, the defendant/broker must have been more than a little surprised to see the plaintiff at the auction, bidding against him. Surely one of the things he would say in his defense would be that had he thought of the matter, he would certainly have precluded this possibility explicitly in the contract. He would say he had not thought of it just because it seemed so obvious. And once again we have the vagueness inherent in establishing the system of background expectations, in establishing the context of an agreement.

Lon Fuller liked to cite an example from Wittgenstein, in which someone told to "show the children a game" teaches them a game involving gambling with dice.[32] Not only contractual arrangements but words, phrases, and sentences have a system of background expectations, which cannot be specified in full beforehand, and whose limitations become apparent only when somebody transgresses them. Just as a word, phrase, or sentence must be understood in context—not all of which will be specified—so must a contractual undertaking. The question that arises is the same question we considered in chapter 5: Is this system of background expectations, this context, susceptible to a factual, cognitively identifiable specification, or is it normative? I would concede that here, just as in the general case of language, this system of background expectations can hardly be specified by a system of necessary and sufficient conditions, in principle identifiable beforehand. One sometimes may not know what is included in the system until the question arises. This makes the specification of meaning look like a matter of choice rather than understanding, and choice, of course, is governed by values, norms. Thus a dichotomy is set up between matters of fact on one hand, which are supposed to be ascertainable at least in principle by noncontroversial, ideally mechanical routines, and matters of value, which relate to choice and are in principle arbitrary. This is a false dichotomy. It is possible to call something a matter of understanding, even though its actual results cannot have been specified beforehand in terms of necessary and sufficient conditions. And so the determination of what fits under a value concept is not *just* a matter of choice. The fact that we cannot, for example, be said to know beforehand all instances of what counts as cruel behavior does not mean that our designation of a novel instance as true cruelty is an arbitrary decision. There is an element of understanding, and the concept of cruelty itself determines our decision, though we cannot fully know that determination beforehand.

Thus the liberal conception of contract is made to look inadequate by having foisted upon it an untenable conception of language. Promises, like every human expression, are made against an unexpressed background of shared purposes, experiences, and even a shared theory of the world. Without such a common background communication would be impossible. Of course the congruence of background between two persons is never more than partial, but only the solipsist draws pessimistic conclusions from that. What is at once obvious and remarkable is the extent to which practical and quite profound interchange is possible. In conversation, a myriad of testing clues — sometimes as minute as missed eye contact — allow the parties to sense when communication between them is not succeeding, so that they must adjust, reformulate, make explicit what otherwise might have been left implicit, and so finally allow them to reestablish communication against a more general shared context. The absence of such clues may explain why highly limited exchanges, such as the exchange of letters in *Raffles v. Wichelhaus* about the ship *Peerless*, can easily go wrong no matter how fully the parties share a common "consciousness". And we can also see the absurdity of the desire of some classical contract theorists to limit the interpretive scrutiny of the promise to the four corners of the document itself. This fatuity is related to the doctrine of letting the loss lie where it falls, discussed in chapter 5.

There is no need for parties to agree in advance or to want the same thing in order to be able to understand each other and to reach agreement. There is always some deeper, more general level of shared experience and striving to which appeal can be made in order to make the particular project mutually intelligible. With mutual intelligibility the stage is set for an exchange of promises. And this is crucial to a proper, uninflated view of the concept of good faith. For the possibility of mutual comprehension shows that good faith requires not loyalty to some undefined relationship but only loyalty to the promise itself — the faithful carrying out of the mutual promises that the parties, having come to understand their *separate* purposes, chose to exchange. This conception of loyalty to the promise disposes once and for all of the idea that contract as promise entails a grudging, mean, or formalistic attitude toward contractual obligation. And it closes the gap between good faith as sincerity and good faith as loyalty. Take the example of the Uniform Commercial Code's suggestion about supply and requirements contracts, as it would apply to the *Neofotistos* case. The suggestion seems extreme that only impending bankruptcy can justify curtailments. A sound resolution requires taking into account the contract's assumption of a background of normal variations in needs and conditions, so that good faith will be seen to enjoin that while business conditions are normal the latitude in the contract's wording may not be used to squeeze an unexpected profit or fresh concessions from the other party. When background conditions change, then the obligations may lapse. That an unprofitable brewery should continue in operation just to supply a farmer with a by-product is obviously absurd and would not have been agreed to by the parties had they thought to mention it, any more than the competitive bidding in *Patterson* would have been authorized.*

As we have seen in the discussion of mistake and impossibility, interpretation may fail to locate a core of agreement, and so at some point we must admit that the contract gives out. In such a case we have nothing to do but to reach for other principles of resolution than promise. These principles include not only principles of fault but of sharing and altruism. If drastic consequences hang in the balance for one or the other party and we are reaching the edges of the actual agreement (and who says the boundary must always be a sharp one—the formalists, whoever they may be), inevitably there will be pressure to avoid pushing both language and one's contractual partner to the wall. This is the principle of civility, which per-

*Great controversy has arisen in recent cases about the implication of a duty of good faith in the termination of employees whose contracts either provide nothing about their duration or are explicitly terminable at the will of the employer. In *Fortune v. National Cash Register Co.*, 373 Mass. 96, 364 N.E.2d 1251 (1977), an employer exercised an explicit "termination at will" clause, firing an employee of twenty-five year's standing the day after his name appeared on a $5,000,000 order. The court found the reason for the firing was to pay Fortune as little as possible of the bonus commissions on this order. The court, implying a duty to terminate only in good faith, awarded damages in an amount sufficient to compensate Fortune for the lost commissions. Such decisions are thought by some to exemplify a movement to give employees, through the doctrine of good faith, job-security rights similar to those created by legislation in other countries. See Note, "Protecting At Will Employees against Wrongful Discharge: The Duty to Terminate Only in Good Faith," 93 *Harv. L. Rev.* 1816 (1980). The *Fortune* case at least requires no such sweeping doctrine to allow justice to be done. We may admit the employer's right to fire his employee without granting his right to withhold the commissions, which a reasonable interpretation of the contract would deem to have been earned. Even those cases which appear to go further, e.g., Monge v. Beebe Rubber Co., 114 N.H. 130, 316 A.2d 549 (1977), are reactions to firings not for business reasons but for reasons of malice, personal harassment, or even extortion. I have no difficulty accommodating the judgment that such actions are wrong and their victims deserve redress. See chapter 2 supra, at 24, and chapter 7 infra, at 103n.

mits the smooth functioning not only of private but of civil institutions: Dubious advantages are not pressed to their limit, lest the willingness to cooperate be undermined and the necessary limitations of language and goodwill be overreached.

Roberto Unger concludes his treatment of contract with a moving peroration on the contrast between Venice and Belmont, the two regions in *The Merchant of Venice* exemplifying the two approaches to contract law. Belmont is the domain of love, of family relations — in short, of altruism. Venice is the domain of commerce, where even the harshest bargain must be kept literally, at no matter what cost in suffering. The liberal vision, according to Unger, keeps these two domains rigidly apart with the rent soul of man commuting uneasily between the two. In his commercial dealings, in his business, and therefore in his public dealings man is governed by the strict regime of contracts, which is unsoftened by any touch of humanity or forebearance. And this is only made tolerable by his ability periodically to retreat to Belmont, a private world of sweetness and light. The contrast is between commercial and family relations, the former governed by the formally realizable, literalistic doctrines of contract, the latter governed by a spirit of sharing and sacrifice.

The contrast is false through and through. Certainly it is true that relations within a family must be governed by an altruistic spirit, a spirit of common purpose, sharing, and sacrifice. A family in which all benefits and burdens were allocated by strict, prior arrangement with readjustments only by some sharply bargained quid pro quo would be a travesty. Yet this proves nothing. For the sharing within a family is and must be voluntary. Where the sharing is mandated by a higher authority it becomes despotism. A despotism may be benign, even necessary, as where parents enforce a regime of forbearance between their young children. But such parental enforcement becomes gradually less tolerable as children grow older. Enforced against late adolescents or adults it is pure tyranny. Between the adult or near-adult members of the family the sharing must come freely. Where the will to share is lacking, then in due course the sounder, healthier instinct dictates that the unit be dissolved.

Nor in commercial relations is there any imperative that contractual partners refuse to share. In fact there are many motives for such sharing in most commercial contexts: from the desire to maintain goodwill so that relations will continue into the future, to a genuinely altruistic concern for one's fellow man, customer, or business partner. Nothing in the liberal concept of contract, nothing in the liberal concept of humanity and law makes such altruism improbable or meaningless. The disposition to view one another with kindness and forbearance is an affirmative good, which liberalism is in no way committed to deny. But, just as in the family, the enforcement of such a posture itself tends to tyranny. Parties enter into contractual relations with certain expectations; for the state to disappoint those expectations is on *its* part a form of tyranny and deception.

# 7

# DURESS
# AND
# UNCONSCIONABILITY

ertain contracts are claimed
to be unfair although the parties entered into them with their eyes
open. The legal doctrines that make this claim are duress and unconscionability. A promise given under duress, though knowingly made,
is not freely made. Paradigmatically, it is a promise induced by the
threat of force (as contrasted to fraud); and by extension it is a promise made in response to any improper pressure. Unconscionability is
a vaguer notion, which concentrates rather on the imbalance, the
substantive unfairness of the agreement itself. High interest rates,
unfair credit terms, low wages, or high prices, and provisions allowing employment or franchises to be terminated at will or severely
limiting warranties in the sale of goods have all been condemned as
unconscionable. In actual legal usage unconscionability is often used

to refer to cognitive as well as substantive defects. For instance, the Uniform Commercial Code—in a confused and confusing provision—speaks of both "unfair surprise" and "oppression," without making clear to what extent these are distinct notions.[1] I have dealt in the preceding chapter with fraud and other forms of taking advantage of cognitive defects, so I put that aspect of unconscionability aside here. Of the three notions—good faith, duress, unconscionability—unconscionability is the most far-reaching, as it suggests that even contracts knowingly and freely made (that is, not in response to improper pressures) may be judged so unfair as not to be binding.

In this chapter I consider whether it is possible to admit the defenses of duress and unconscionability without giving away the heart of my position. Unlike the doctrine of good faith, duress and unconscionability can hardly be used to impose obligations that the parties never assumed. Rather they dispense from obligation. Yet such a dispensing power, if systematically used to effect some extrinsically ordained balance of advantages, can amount to a very general authority over persons and their arrangements. And so here too my task is to show that duress and unconscionability need not be viewed as open-ended invitations to rearrange the understandings people have reached. I must also go further, however, to show that these doctrines perform distinct functions that are not only compatible with the concept of contract as promise but even essential to it.

## DURESS

Duress is a vice in the making of the agreement. Moreover, the vice is not the least bit cognitive: The victim of duress is all too aware of what is happening and what will happen to him. Duress relates not to rationality or cognition but to freedom or volition. Just as contract as promise excludes obligations assumed by people who do not know what they are doing—madmen, people who do not understand the language, people laboring under mistaken assumptions, people who are too confused to understand the significance of their undertakings—so also it excludes cases in which a person's assent is not voluntary.[2] If I am hypnotized into signing a contract or if my hand is moved by another to make a mark signifying assent, I have not promised. Obviously, if the concept of duress covered only such gross instances of involuntary apparent assent it would not be of much interest. In fact duress covers many kinds of situations in which it does not seem right to treat a *knowing* act of agreement as binding because in one way or another it is felt that there was no fair choice. This intuition, however, poses a dilemma for contract doctrine and for the theory of contract as promise, of contract as autonomous self-determination. If a promisor knows what he is doing, if he fully appreciates the alternatives and chooses among them, how can it ever be correct to say that his was not a free choice?[3]

The shrewd and brave man who hands his wallet over to an armed robber makes a calculated decision. The ardent stamp collector faced with a steep price for the remaining "Penny Black" needed to complete his plate block makes a calculated choice. Even the fond uncle who promises to pay for his nephew's trip to Europe makes a choice when faced with this cherished dream of a person whom he wishes to please. Is the promise made under duress in any of these cases? It would be absurd to say that a choice is free enough to ground a promise only if it is in some sense gratuitous or unmotivated.[4] If only unmotivated choices were free, courts would be committed to reviewing on grounds of duress all contractual choices that issued from the parties' goals and desires. If on the other hand duress focuses only on the relative wealth or advantages of the parties to a transaction and disparities in these are held to undermine the voluntariness of the choice, then we might just as well redistribute directly, holding the rich but not the poor to their bargains. Either view is inconsistent with the concept of contract as promise, as autonomy.

The problem is not just theoretical; it is (and has traditionally been seen to be) a make-or-break challenge to the liberal economic theory of the market.[5] For if the market is to be justified on any other than the instrumental ground of leading to the most efficient allocations of resources, it must be because the market is the system of free men freely contracting (promising) with each other. Doubts about the moral status of calculated choices as embodied in bargains (or, as in the case of the uncle's promise, even in gifts), doubts that lead these choices to be validated only if they accord with an external, imposed judgment, undermine the case for the market and the case for promising as well. Thus the law has sought to define duress in formal terms, or at any rate in terms that do not imply a substantive judgment on the choices made.

The standard textbook definition of duress focuses on compulsion by threat.[6] Since threats operate on the will and the response to a threat is a volitional one, the law is immediately faced with the problem I have just described. The first, rather feeble attempt at a resolution holds that only such threats as would overcome the will of a person of ordinary firmness vitiate assent.[7] I suppose the kind of case envisaged is one where a person is threatened with the torture of a loved one. This formula imagines a threat so strong that the very power of choice, of calculation, is put into question. It seeks to avoid the impending problem by extending the notion of physical coercion to some kind of psychological coercion. Though one might readily accept this extension, it obviously covers too little ground, and the need to go beyond it was early appreciated. For instance, it does not cover the robber's threat; it would not cover the threat to burn down my house if I did not accede to a particular agreement.

## Coercion and Rights

Consider three cases:

I. An armed robber threatens his victim on a dark and lonely street: "Your money or your life."

II. One of many competing supermarkets in an affluent suburb offers shoppers peas at thirty-nine cents a can.

III. One stamp collector offers another a "Penny Black" at a steep price, knowing that the buyer needs just this stamp to complete a set.

Duress is clearly present in the first and absent in the second case. A natural and familiar way to distinguish the two and to probe the third case is in terms of the concept of coercion. The victim's acquiescence in the first case is coerced; the purchase of the can of peas is not. What distinction is being marked, and how does it apply to the stamp collector? Robert Nozick, in a philosophical discussion of coercion, distinguishes among threats, offers, and warnings, proposing that only the first are coercive.*[8] A threat worsens the recipient's situation; he would rather not have received it. An offer at least leaves the offeree indifferent and generally improves his situation by increasing his options. The robber plainly issues a threat, the grocer

---

*The focus on threats is sound, as gestures that are physically compelled — the hand that is forced to mark an X on a document — do not count as actions at all. And warnings are beside the point, as the warner merely informs of a state of affairs that he cannot or will not change, whatever the other party's response.

and stamp dealer make offers. As Nozick acknowledges, however, this distinction requires further refinement.

IV. Pickles, who owns land beneath which flows an underground stream, proposes to block off this stream unless promised payment by the borough of Bradford, which needs the stream to improve its water supply.[9]

V. A landowner, a remote corner of whose land has been used for a period of years (though less time than necessary to establish a right of way) as a convenient short cut, bars this path and refuses to reopen it unless paid.

VI. A student pianist who has given free annual recitals in his village church for several years announces that henceforth he will require a fee.

VII. An enterprising journalist discovers that a professor of moral philosophy was convicted of embezzlement years ago. He proposes to publish this fact in a review of the professor's new book, unless the professor promises to pay him several thousand dollars.

These cases show that the distinction between proposals that worsen another's situation (threats) and those which may improve it by increasing options (offers) leaves open the question of how the recipient's prior situation is identified. It would be nice if the benchmark for determining whether a proposal worsens the situation or not could be a purely factual one. In case I this would yield a clear answer, but in cases IV-VII there are different ways of describing the status quo.

The stream had been flowing all along, the path was there and used, and so Pickles and the landowner may be said to be proposing to change the status quo for the worse. In the case of the pianist, however, one does not know what to say. Is the status quo what obtained just before the day of the annual concert arrived, so that his giving the concert would be an improvement? Or is the status quo defined as including an *annual* concert? We may be of two minds about Pickles's or the landowner's proposals, but few would find the pianist's proposal coercive or in any other way objectionable. Notice that it does no good to shift from a static status quo (the situation the instant just before the proposal) to a dynamic status quo where one speaks more largely of interfering with the normal course of events, for in the normal course of events the concert pianist would have played and the journalist published—yet the pianist proposes an ordinary market transaction, the journalist proposes blackmail. Might we not say, then, that it is coercive to elicit a promise by threatening *harm*? But equating coercion with a proposal to do harm (as opposed to refusing to benefit) runs into analogous difficulties. Would Pickles harm the town by stopping the flow of water? By putting a chain across the path does the landowner do harm to the would-be users? Does the pianist "stop" his concerts, thereby harming the villagers, or does he just refuse to confer a benefit? Finally, even the idea of harming *maliciously*, using another's harm as your chosen means of getting what you want, will not do the trick: Pickles and the landowner propose to go to some trouble just in order to deprive others of a benefit. The pianist may want to play and may propose to stay at home just in an attempt to get his fee. The proposal is strategic in each case. And in the case of the blackmailer, the change proposed is to *avoid* a harm which he would otherwise inflict in the normal course.

These conundrums should be sufficient to show that we cannot escape using some normative criterion to distinguish offers from threats. And that is a pity since the purpose of the inquiry is itself normative: to identify coercion and thus to determine which promises (and contracts) are not morally (or legally) binding. It is always neater if a moral conclusion can be made to turn directly on non-moral criteria, for when the moral depends on the moral there is always the danger of a vicious circle. And of course there are those who believe that calling a contract coerced does no more than announce our decision not to enforce it. But if a moral criterion is deeper, more general, or at any rate independent of the moral issue it determines, then there is no circularity at all. It is that deeper though moral criterion for coercion which we must look for.

A proposal is not coercive if it offers what the proponent has a right to offer or not as he chooses. It is coercive if it proposes a wrong to the object of the proposal.[10]

The robber has no right to inflict the harm he threatens; he would wrong his victim. The grocer has a right to offer the can of peas at whatever price he chooses, and the shopper has no right to take them without paying the price. Thus, the status quo that the proposal alters is defined in terms of the rights of the parties. Though passersby had used the landowner's path, they had no right to—they had been trespassing. If they can trespass no longer their rights have not been diminished. On the contrary; for the first time they enjoy the prospect of being able to use the path legally, if only they pay for the privilege.*

The success of this criterion of coercion will depend on whether it is possible to fix a conception of what is right and what is wrong, of what rights people have in contractual relations independently of whether their contracts should be enforced. Indeed the violation of such an independent norm must necessarily undermine the validity of a promise obtained by its violation. Let us posit an independent norm N such that to do n to a person violates that person's rights. Assume a person procures a promise by threatening to do n to the promisor, who later refuses to keep his promise. The promisee can scarcely be heard to complain that he has been cheated, that he forbore to do n (inflict injury on a robbery victim, for instance) in return for a promise now broken. In a legal forum such a claim would be absurd. Nor may the promisee complain of the promisor's immorality, his breach of faith. For (as I argued in chapters 2 and 3) though an exchange is not necessary to the obligation of a promise where a promise is in fact part of an exchange, the trust relationship is intended to be mutual if it is to exist at all. To recognize such an exchange-promise as binding—legally or morally—is to acknowledge the validity of the exchange and thus to deny that the exchange threatens the promisor's rights. If the promisor is condemned as acting wrongly in breaking his promise, is the promisee now released from his reciprocal obligation? What would that mean? Would it now be permissible to do n, to violate norm N? That would mean that if the threat is successful it does away with the norm.**

So I conclude that a promise procured by a threat to do wrong to

---

*I only seem to be using the terms "rights," "right," and "wrong" indiscriminately. If I have a right, then I do no wrong when I exercise it, and you do me wrong if you violate that right. If a person wrongs another, he violates the victim's right not to have this wrong inflicted on him. To say a person has no right to do something is ambiguous. It may just mean that he has what in law is called a liberty—he does no wrong in doing that thing, but he is not wronged if prevented. But in ordinary speech the locution has the stronger sense that to do that thing is itself wrong. See *Right and Wrong* chs. 4 and 5.

**This last point is related to the familiar moral dilemma of whether it is permissible to lie to an assassin in search of his victim. Augustine and Kant hold lying to be absolutely wrong and so deny the propriety of such a lie. I follow Benjamin Constant in the argument that the assassin has forfeited the right not to be lied to in that case. See *Right and Wrong* ch. 3.

the promisor, a threat to violate his rights, is without moral force. It is such threats that constitute the legal category of duress.

## Property

Those who see contract law as just a device of social policy, whether of redistribution or of efficiency, and who argue that the doctrine of duress is just a way of redistributing advantages in pursuit of social policy, are not likely to be stopped by my formulation of the issue. For them the assignment of rights simply reflects the desired policy judgment. Now the argument that the condemnation of physical threats (as by the robber) reflects a redistributive judgment is if anything more absurd than the similar argument about deception examined in chapter 6. Intentional violence (and so the threat of it) to the person of another is wrong, irrespective of the overall balance of advantage between the assailant and his victim. To be sure, condemning such violence and granting a right not to be its victim does affect the balance of advantage between the two parties, but that is not the basis of the condemnation. It has also been argued that such a condemnation leads to a more efficient allocation of resources.[11] The correctness and even the coherence of that claim are open to question, but even granting the point, this does not show that efficiency is the basis of the moral condemnation. As I have sought to show elsewhere[12] the condemnation of intentional violence is more firmly rooted in moral notions of respect for persons and the physical basis of personality. The right to be free of such violence expresses the judgment that our persons (and thus our physical persons) are not available to be used by others against our will. This same idea helps to explain the case of the pianist. (Case VI). To deny him the right to dispose of his labor and talent on whatever terms he chooses is to assert that the townspeople have rights to them also, so that his proposal to withhold his performance becomes a threat to deprive the townspeople of their due. But a person's right to his own person and thus to his talents and efforts is a fundamental tenet of liberal individualism, not just a passing, contingent judgment designed to effect some particular economic or social scheme under particular circumstances. Thus that the robber's contract is void for duress and that the pianist's is not can be determined by a notion of right and wrong that is quite independent of the contractual issues it resolves.

The same is not obviously true of Pickles's case (IV). In the case of the stamp dealer (III) it seems natural enough (though there are problems here too) to say that if the "Penny Black" is his, he does no wrong in offering it for sale at whatever price the traffic will bear. Pickles's ownership of his land, however, does not obviously carry with it the right to block off the underground stream. And once we push this doubt we see that the case of the shortcut (V) is clear only by stipulation: Had the neighbors used the path for a few years more or had the period for acquiring a prescriptive right been defined as being a few years less, the landowner's demand would have been as extortionate as that of the blackmailing journalist—of which more also must be said. In fact, though Pickles won his case in 1895 in England, the law in the United States generally forbids malicious or even unreasonable action by a landowner to stop up percolating waters.[13] And when we move above ground, we are reminded by Morton Horwitz[14] that the legal regime governing the right to divert streams flowing through or by your land has been subject to the greatest variability: English law differs from American, and American law has changed too, in response—claims Horwitz—to changing intellectual and political currents and changing perceptions of the needs of the economy. The point is, of course, that rules of property are very largely conventional.

If promise is defeated by duress, and duress is equated with coercion, and coercion is a threat to violate rights, and property is a source of right, and the nature and extent of property are conventional, and the conventions of property are drawn or develop to serve the community's (efficiency or redistributive) goals,[15] why then it seems to follow that the obligation of promise itself is the creature of community, not individual, will.[16] This chain of reasoning is, however, linked together by two crucial fallacies.

*First*, not all property is conventional.[17] The grounds for recognizing a (property) right in one's own person, talent, and efforts are nonconventional in the sense that they are part of moral theory—liberal individualism, but other moral theories as well—and so depend not on arguments of social expediency but on the truth of the moral theory. If that is what is meant by natural law, then such rights are natural. (This is the analogue to the point, made in chapter 6, that certain rules of fraud, like the prohibitions against lying and against violating certain relations of trust, depend on moral, not just conventional standards.)

*Second*, even those rights which are conventional — such as the rights to percolating waters — are conventional *rights*. By casting the relation between a person and a thing in this form of a right, we withdraw it *pro tanto* from the domain of collective imposition.[18] To say that the collector's "Penny Black" is *his* assimilates that relation to the relation between a man and what is quintessentially his, namely, his person, his effort, his talents. Now I do not deny that property rights are defined in part to accomplish social ends. What the collectivist argument misses is that these collective ends are accomplished by creating *rights*, by granting individuals discretionary control, a private sphere of activity. Some political theorists like Adam Smith and Friedrich Hayek[19] argue that collective goals are in fact best achieved by enlisting individual initiative through a regime of rights. I am not persuaded that this is so, and I am persuaded that even if it were so this argument would not be the sole ground for proceeding in this way. The regime of property rights represents a compromise between collective concerns (which determine the specific contours of property rights) and a respect for individuals, whose collaboration is enlisted on the understanding that they retain the measure of discretion that any right implies. Indeed, to withdraw all relations to things from the regime of rights would render largely nugatory the natural right to one's own person and efforts, for those efforts are expended on the outside world.[20]

Nor is the changeability of property rights an insurmountable obstacle, so long as changes are gradual or prospective.[21] A sharp change in definition amounts to confiscation.[22] It is a dishonest procedure, which succeeds only by preying on the confidence of individuals — like a government that on the eve of a currency devaluation issues reassuring denials of its imminent intentions. A sophistic argument based on the changeable, varied, and conventional nature of property rights seeks to avoid this charge of collective bad faith by defining every property right at the outset to include a liability to have that right drastically diminished at any time at the collectivity's discretion.[23] Such a proposal is too clever by half. To be sure, a right must have boundaries, and those boundaries may be temporal as well as spatial, or conceptual and conditional as well as temporal or spatial, but if the condition is so broad that in reality the right is wholly at the discretion of others, then it is no right at all. This is a matter of degree, but there is a right just to the degree that a domain of discretion—temporal, spatial, and conceptual—is granted to the individual.*

Test these generalities against the case of the black-mailing journalist (VII). What is so offensive about his conduct; why are we so clear that a promise made to him need not be kept? Is it because he, like the robber, proposes to do harm rather then offers a benefit, so that there is something malicious about his conduct? As we have seen, this reasoning will not work, since Pickles (IV), the landowner (V), and the pianist (VII) propose to do something—if *not* playing when you would be glad to play is doing something—that will cause harm in order to extract payment. Yet the malice does seem to play a role. In condemning blackmail we exclude the use of property (including property in one's effort) for the general purpose of harming others; we exclude investments in the *harmful* potential of things, effort, or talent. The use of land as a shortcut is in general a beneficial use; the pianist's development of his talent leads to benefit. Granting a property right in these cases permits the benefit to be withheld, but the blackmailer's initial investment is in a potential harm. Even the first time the law judged a contract with a blackmailer to have been made under duress should not have been a surprise. Such a decision was not unprincipled, but applied a pervasive community judgment that investments in the misery of others should not be lucrative. It would be possible also to distinguish case VII from one in which the journalist did his research, fully intending to publish it, and then asked, in return for his silence, only what he would lose by not publishing. After all, why should not the motive figure in judging whether the journalist's conduct was wrong? (Only the formalist would insist that such judgments must issue algorithmically from explicit prior rules, and, as I have argued, formalism is a position to which the liberal theory of contract is in no way committed.) Motive might also be used in Pickles's case, distinguishing a landowner's right to use percolating waters for any purpose of his own, even if he thereby excludes others, from a right to exclude others just in order to extract payment. A distinction of that sort, however, is more conventional, more instrumental than natural (compared to the case of the blackmailer), and for that

---

*I put aside the question of emergencies. That they may be (and regularly have been) invoked by governments in bad faith whenever rights have proven inconvenient does not mean that their invocation in good faith vitiates my argument. So also changed circumstances may alter the terms of the compact between citizen and government in ways analogous to those discussed in chapter 6 supra.

reason fairness requires that it be more clearly tied to prior, available rulings.*

## HARD BARGAINS

The decided cases do not invoke the doctrine of unconscionability in any systematic or even coherent way. Claims of substantive unfairness are mixed with suggestions of fraud, cognitive deficiency, and duress, so that it is not possible to discern a pattern in the factual situations in which this episodic dispensing power is exercised. Certain leading cases do, however, represent distinct tendencies in the law. I use them in this section as a point of departure for my own substantive proposals.

### Unconscionability, Economic Duress, and Social Justice

Consider these cases:

VII. Retailer in a low-income, inner-city area offers major appliances for sale at much higher prices than are available at de-

*Let us assume that a right of way or a stream does indeed belong to the landowner to do with as he wishes. May he deny them, block them off, *not* to enforce even a very hard bargain, but to spite a particular person who wishes to use them? For that matter, may a workman refuse to work even at what he considers a splendid wage for someone he does not like? I see no difficulty in arguing that it is immoral, wrong, under some circumstances to deprive an innocent person, because of hatred or contempt, of an advantage you would be willing to grant others. Such hatred or contempt is in itself a moral injury, unless justified by the other person's conduct, and even then there are limits to the appropriate response. It is immoral to discriminate among people without reason, and to treat some as less worthy of respect. That being the case, there is no reason in principle why one could not also condemn as wrong a refusal to enter into contractual relations that is based on immoral attitudes of hatred and contempt. There is nothing in individualism or in the theory of autonomy that justifies such attitudes. Cf. *American Law of Property*, supra note 13; Hayek, supra note 19, at 135-137.

The difficulties in basing legal conclusions on this moral judgment are only practical — but these practical difficulties are great. We would be willing to grant, for instance, that a worker might find association with other workers more agreeable, that a person might find the company of some people more pleasant than that of others. If the attitudes on which such discriminations are based do not involve attitudes of contempt — as for instance in cases of racial hatred — there is no moral objection to a worker being willing to labor for less in the company of his friends and therefore only for more in the company of strangers. So the moral judgment is a complex one. In fact the law seeks to take account of these complexities, while recognizing its practical limitations. For instance, in antidiscrimination housing laws exceptions are usually made for owner-occupied premises, perhaps not so much because racial hatred is justified in such contexts as out of an unwillingness to intrude the rather blunt instrument of the law into matters of personal association. The more unlikely it is that justifiable discriminations are present, the more willing the law is to enforce a regime of impartiality. But of course none of this undercuts the notion that a person may seek to obtain his best price through bargaining and through threatening to withhold benefits unless he receives a price he considers acceptable.

partment stores and discount houses. Retailer offers credit to customers many of whom are not regularly employed and would not be granted credit through normal channels. The credit terms are exorbitant: interest rates are high, security is retained in all goods purchased, and the goods are repossessed after even trivial defaults. A welfare recipient, who has purchased furniture, a stove, a refrigerator , and an air conditioner and paid more than two-thirds of the charges, defaults, and the retailer seeks to repossess everything. The resale value of the used items is so low that it will not even cover the remaining debt.[24]

IX. A small contractor specializing in exterior repairs offers jobs at low wages to young men in a time of high unemployment. He explains that the work is dangerous and that he has limited safety equipment and limited insurance coverage. Each employee signs an undertaking to accept the full risk of the work and under no circumstances to sue for injuries. An employee falls from a shaky ladder, of whose condition he was clearly aware, and is seriously injured. He sues, claiming that employer was negligent and had not furnished a safe place to work. (Put aside, for the moment, that workmen's compensation laws would today make such an action generally both impossible and unnecessary.)[25]

X. All automobile manufacturers agree among themselves to offer a standard warranty, excluding any liability for personal injuries caused by defective manufacture or design. A purchaser is injured by a poorly designed steering wheel and seeks recovery.[26]

In cases like these, some courts have refused to enforce promises, finding their terms to be unconscionable.[27] The reasoning behind such decisions comes down to this: The promisor had no real choice *and* the actual terms are substantially unfair to him, particularly in view of his poverty or relative powerlessness.* The "no real choice" locution is obviously unsatisfactory on its own to explain these decisions, since any consumer facing a perfectly competitive market for some necessity or set of necessities has no real choice but to pay the market price; just as the producers have no real choice but to accept that price. The substantive unfairness claim is also opaque; it is in-

---

*A lack of confidence in the soundness of this reasoning is shown by the fact that a hint of cognitive defect — like the Uniform Commercial Code's reference to unfair surprise — is generally thrown into the explanation, but not clearly or definitely enough to make it seem worthwhile to ask whether the promisor really was surprised or whether such surprise is a necessary element. See Leff, supra note 1, at 497-501.

conceivable, for instance, that a court would strike down the stamp collector's bargain on the ground that the price was outrageously high. The focus is on necessities: A car or a job is a necessity. What needs probing is the notion of substantive unfairness. Analysis reveals it to be two parts sentiment and one part common sense.

How far we are prepared to condemn the apparently rapacious merchant (VIII) or employer (IX) should depend on further circumstances. Suppose that the far greater frequency of default made high prices and harsh credit terms a necessity for doing business with an often nearly destitute clientele;[28] suppose that the small contractor would not be able to stay in business at all and that his laborers would remain unemployed if he had to pay higher wages, use better equipment, or assume (that is, insure against) the risk of accidents. On these assumptions the charge of unfairness seems sentimental and not a little unjust. Both the merchant and the employer are offering their supposed "victims" further options, enlarging their opportunities; if the alternatives seem harsh, that is a misfortune for which none of the parties to these contracts is responsible.* Is it still wrong to "prey" on that misfortune? More sentiment comes in with that question. What would be the effect of indulging that sentiment and condemning those contracts as unconscionable? The destitute consumer would be spared one more pain and humiliation in a life full of them. The young laborer would be provided for in his disability and maybe just this once the reversal of their expectations would drive neither entrepreneur out of business. But the judgment cannot be limited to "just this once." If each businessman is operating at the margin (either of bankruptcy or of the point where some alternative use of his effort and capital is preferred) then such a judgment must be a signal to cut losses and close up shop. Well, maybe we *want* to defeat his expectations and to move the businessman a little closer to the situation of the poor people he appears to exploit. But that too is a confused judgment. Why should just this one representative of the more fortunate classes be made to bear the burden of our redistributive zeal? Surely not because he happened to seek his opportunities in offering increased options to the poor. Presumably we want the poor to be able to buy refrigerators on

---

*Sometimes it is said that poor people do not understand contractual provisions or are unable to calculate risks rationally. Such arguments are often patronizing as well as paternalistic. Where they are valid, the doctrine of mistake offers some relief. See chapter 5 supra. So also does legislation requiring detailed and understandable explanations and a period of time for reflection.

credit; we want unskilled workers to have a chance to work. The judgment of unconscionability in such circumstances would be another instance of the social fraud that I pointed out in regard to switching the rules of disclosure defining fraud or the rules of right and wrong defining duress. For society gets what it wants—increased opportunities for the poor—by enlisting investments on terms it will not honor.

This conclusion makes the promise principle (and liberal political morality) seem harsh and insensitive to the situation of the less fortunate, until we recall that liberal political theory (and practice) accept distributive justice as a goal of collective action, but one to be pursued by the collectivity as a whole, funded by the general contributions of all citizens. Redistribution is not a burden to be borne in a random, ad hoc way by those who happen to cross paths with persons poorer than themselves. Such a conception, heartwarmingly spontaneous though it may be, would in the end undermine our ability to plan and to live our lives as we choose. Liberal democracies have chosen to effect redistribution (to assure a social minimum) by welfare benefits on one hand and by general taxation based on overall ability to pay on the other.[29] In this way government, as it seeks contributions to remove inequalities, remains neutral about the ways in which the better-off acquire their greater wealth, exacting (in principle, at least) the same contribution from everyone who enjoys the same level of wealth. Thus the retailer and the employer in our examples would pay taxes depending on the profits of their businesses. Those taxes in turn would (or should) go to reduce the poverty and to remedy the conditions that make inner-city consumers such poor credit risks and unskilled laborers so desperate for even ill-paid, dangerous work. But there is no reason why the retailer or employer should assume more of a burden in this regard than, say, a Beverly Hills plastic surgeon with ten times their income, just because the surgeon never has occasion to deal with the poor and unemployed. Thus though the general conditions that give rise to the contracts in cases VIII and IX may be unfair, it is unfair (and in the end counterproductive) to force particular persons, who are making their private arrangements against the background of conditions they did not create, to bear the burden of remedying these conditions. The provision of a just social minimum should be society's general responsibility, not the responsibility of individual economic actors, except as they pay taxes to fund that minimum.

This is the liberal principle, but it assumes a well-functioning market and hardships caused only by the relative poverty of the parties and by general resource constraints. These ideal conditions never obtain completely and sometimes are so far from obtaining that serious distortions result. It may be, for instance, that difficulties of entry, the small number of competitors, the concentration of producers versus the dispersal of consumers, allow the automobile manufacturers in case X by their cartel-like agreement to lower the cost of accidents to themselves at the expense of consumers and thus to enjoy a monopoly profit—that is, a profit greater than is necessary to enlist an optimum level of investment in automobile manufacturing. By refusing to enforce the no-warranty clause, we force automobile manufacturers to give up their monopoly profits to consumers, and the result will be greater economic efficiency—manufacturers will be moved to manufacture more or safer cars at the lower price.[30] A decision for the injured driver, thus, is not sentimental in the sense that we indulge an impulse of the moment while refusing to affirm its systematic consequences. On the contrary, the systematic consequences of the decision are just what we want.

Now it might be that ignorance, fear, and prejudice constitute as effective barriers to competition as high capital costs, so that perhaps the retailer in VIII and the employer in XI, far from providing a market service at a market price are in fact exploiting a natural monopoly. It may be, for instance, that low-cost, high-volume merchants could perfectly well do business in inner-city slums and on much less onerous terms than those set out in VIII. If we allow retailer a high profit, we reward him for seeing and seizing the opportunity. So why should we not "reward" the automobile manufacturers for seizing theirs? (Indeed, respecting property rights in any scarce resource—including talent and enterprise—will confer some measure of monopoly status on the right-holder.) But there is a crucial difference: By their agreement (conspiracy in restraint of trade) the automobile manufacturers create and maintain monopoly conditions; the retailer and small contractor do nothing of the sort. The automobile manufacturers' kind of conspiracy can be proscribed by general rules beforehand. But there is no way to distinguish the advantage taken by the enterprising retailer or employer from that enjoyed by the inventor of the hula hoop except that they draw their profit from the poor—and that alone, I have argued, is not a reason to strike down their bargains as unconscionable. If poverty is what creates their opportunities, then only curing poverty will remedy what displeases us about their arrangements. The arrangements themselves are blameless.*

Bankruptcy laws offer an apparent exception to this principle that redistribution should be a social burden, not one imposed episodically on individuals as they come into contractual relations with particular poor people. These laws—with their system of exemptions and exclusions, going back perhaps to the abolition of imprisonment for debt—provide that no matter what a man's contractual obligations, he will not be disabled from supporting himself and his family at some reasonable level. He will neither be disabled by threats (such as imprisonment for debt) if he does not hand over his earnings, nor by an attachment of these minimal earnings, nor by an attachment of the necessities (food, clothing, minimal furnishings, and shelter) they buy.**31 This might be viewed as a case where the *social* minimum is provided not out of *social* resources, but rather at the expense of particular contractual partners whose full contractual rights are not recognized—as if it were indeed unconscionable to exact "a pound of flesh" from a promisor in desperate straits. Far from being an anomaly, the regime of exclusions in bankruptcy accords well with a system of public assistance. Nobody suggests, for instance, that public assistance payments should go to pay off contractual liabilities. But if public assistance implies a floor beyond which people will not be allowed to sink, so that one cannot look to a contractual partner's welfare payments to meet contractual obligations, it is not a long step to hold that in fact the courts will not push a person to a point where he requires public assistance. True, the "burden" of this policy does fall on a particular individual, but it does so in a way not unlike fraud, theft, and natural catastrophy. Indeed, contractual partners generally treat bankruptcy as a risk to

*I put to one side rules that, for instance, forbid the exclusion of certain warranties, or (as in the case of certain insurance contracts) require the inclusion of standard clauses, or regulate certain businesses or relations by setting mandatory safety standards or requiring workmen's compensation insurance. First, these are general, usually legislative rules. Second, they are often designed to remove specific market imperfections. Third, many (like minimum wage laws) may be ineffectual or counterproductive.

**Where a contractual obligation forbids competition with a former employer, even this will not be enforced if the effect of enforcement is to deprive a worker of his ability to earn a living in his usual occupation. See *Restatement* (2d) §330(1); 6 Corbin §1394, pp. 101-104; Harlan M. Blake, "Employee Agreements Not to Compete," 73 *Harv. L. Rev.* 625 (1960); G. Kreider, "Trends in the Enforcement of Restrictive Employment Contracts," 35 *U. Cin. L. Rev.* 16 (1966).

the successful conclusion of their ventures. Is this an example of altruism? There is no doubt that it is—but a very general, clearly defined, and circumscribed one.

## Bad Samaritans

Some bargains, though they meet all of the tests I have set out so far, seem just too hard to enforce. Consider these cases:

XI. In *Post v. Jones*[32] two whaling vessels came upon a disabled third whaler in remote waters some five thousand miles from the nearest port. Being empty themselves, they held an "auction" and took off the helpless vessel's full cargo of oil at a small fraction of its landed value. The Supreme Court of the United States upset this enforced sale, and limited the two rescuers to the normally allowed fee for salvage.

XII. In *Batsakis v. Demotsis*[33] the defendant, desperate for money soon after the German occupation of Greece, borrowed an amount of Greek currency, which in those chaotic circumstances may have been the equivalent of as little as fifty dollars, against her promise to repay two thousand dollars plus normal interest from funds she controlled in the United States. The Supreme Court of Texas enforced the agreement according to its terms.

These bargains *are* offensive to decency, and they differ in an important way from those I have just been discussing. The retailer and his poor customers deal against the background of a functioning social system, which has the power and responsibility to distribute wealth and provide a social minimum. If this responsibility has been discharged reasonably well, then the deal the parties make simply reflects the economic situation that that conception of social justice sanctions. And if the requirements of social justice have not been met (though the political system is democratic), then the responsibility of each citizen is to work politically for a greater measure of social justice. No private citizen, however, has the duty to seek to remedy these systemic inequities on an individual basis and at the sacrifice of his private (as opposed to political) advantage—any more than a judge is entitled to force such episodic altruism by declaring the particular contract unconscionable. But these two last cases pose a different issue. In *Post v. Jones* the relative weakness of the disabled ship is not sanctioned by some general social dispensation. It is a random event, an accident for which (in those days, let us assume) no systematic provision could be made. In *Batsakis v. Demotsis* the social order has melted away at the onslaught of a barbaric invader. Even the minimal conditions of social peace, stability, and concern needed to ratify individual transactions are missing.

As I have argued in detail elsewhere,[34] it is an incorrect conception of liberal individualism to exclude from it any duty to be concerned about and to assist others. The argument has been clear for liberals at least from Kant that indifference to one's fellows devalues our common humanity and so endangers the moral basis for the respect we claim as individuals.[35] If liberalism is distinctive as a moral position, it is in its attempt to accommodate this duty of altruism to an individual's right to define and pursue his own conception of the good without being consumed by the needs of others. The political system of social redistribution I have alluded to several times is a crucial part of that accommodation. As we have seen, it leaves contract as promise quite intact. But sometimes that accommodation fails—either because human foresight cannot provide for every detail, or because human wickedness and lawlessness destroy the complex structure that embodies it. In such cases we might as well be in a state of nature, and in that state our duty of humanity is a duty to help the stranger in distress. In *Post v. Jones* the randomness of the situation guarantees that the imposition will not be too burdensome. And since it arises from a gap in an otherwise well-functioning system, it is reasonable to expect fair compensation, when after the storm we have all reached port—literally and metaphorically.[36] In *Batsakis* the catastrophe is more total, and the duty to help more costly. But since without civil society individual rights are practically worthless, it is not surprising that our common bonds should be particularly demanding in a situation of impending barbarism: By affirming them, we also affirm the hope that civility will not be extinguished and civil society will return.

The rescuers in *Post* had a duty to help and Batsakis had a duty to share with his destitute countrymen. (*Pace* the Supreme Court of Texas.) While there are grave problems about legal enforcement of such duties,[37] there are no such problems about denying legal recognition to promises exacted in return for the performance of what the promisee was bound to do anyway. And so by a straightforward application of the principle set out earlier in this chapter, we see that those promises were exacted under duress. (One is reminded of the blackmailing architect in case VIII in chapter 3.) We may hesitate to grant an affirmative action against one who fails to act as a good Samaritan. We need not hesitate at all to deny the bad Samaritan his unjust profit.

# 8

# THE IMPORTANCE OF BEING RIGHT

**C**ontract law is often highly technical; large consequences turn on what to a nonlawyer may seem to be small differences. Surely this is why so many, both lawyers and nonlawyers, doubt that contract law can really be the expression of moral principle. In this chapter I explore some of these intricate and perhaps surprising doctrines, and show that far from being the perverse inventions of lawyers they are entailments of the promise principle. Promises are self-imposed. They are intended to mark a clear difference between what is undertaken and what would otherwise have obtained. Therefore a person who can claim the benefit of the promissory principle will often enjoy a great advantage, while a person who forfeits that benefit may be remitted to much less advantageous principles of remedy. The shift from one principle to another may make a large difference in the result. That should not be surprising, since by promising, people seek to make major shifts. The natural expression of the promise principle in contract law is the disposition to hold a promisor to his word, to make him do what he has promised—or pay the equivalent of the promised performance. Whether a person's situation, his rights and duties, are controlled by promise or by the surrounding, nonconsensual principles of tort and restitution will make a large difference, since it is the function of promises to alter that situation and of contract law to translate promissory obligation into reality.

Critics of the promise principle have found theoretical support for their attacks in the sometimes abrupt reversals of fortune that the principle brings about. Instrumentalists of every sort—whether economists or those moved by a vague altruistic or socializing attitude—tend to abhor such sharp peripeties.[1] If we take autonomy seriously as a principle for ordering human affairs, however, people must abide by the consequences of their choices, and this imperative will give the ensuing outcomes a discontinuous, binary quality. Whether or not a person has promised is a yes or no question. If he has, he is judged by the regime of promise. If he has not, some other regime controls. And if a person has given a promise and received one in return, his repudiation of his promissory obligations will deprive him of the title to insist that his own claims be judged under that promissory regime. It is crucial to be in the right.

## YOU CAN ALWAYS GET YOUR MONEY BACK

Consider this case:

I. Dealer expects to buy a specified number of large, poor-mileage luxury sedans ("gas guzzlers"). Since it is nearing the end of the model year, he advertises a "special" on these and obtains full payment of $8,000 from Customer on a sedan of this type—the color and optional extras to be specified at a later date. Customer is glad to make this deal, because these cars ordinarily list at close to $10,000. Prior to the date for delivery two things happen: (1) gasoline rationing is instituted, and (2) the model is prematurely discontinued, so that Dealer is unable to obtain any. Because of gasoline rationing the going retail price of comparable "gas guzzlers" falls to the vicinity of $6,000. Customer seeks to get his full $8,000 back.

Both common sense and the law clearly hold that Customer can get his money back, even though if Dealer had kept his side of the bargain, Customer would be worse off, would suffer a $2,000 loss.[2] Or consider a version of the *Security Stove* case set out in chapter 2 as case IV. In the actual case the stove company recovered its reliance losses after Railway Express failed to pick up and deliver the model stove that was to be exhibited at a convention. If the stove company had prepaid the express charges, then there is no doubt that it could have recovered this payment even if Railway Express could have shown that the exhibit would have been a complete failure (a showing that would have defeated the stove company's claim for reliance damages). It seems so obvious that the car buyer and the stove company should get their money back in these cases that we may too easily overlook some problems with this conclusion. To bring them out consider another case:

> II.  Builder is under contract to build a house for Speculator at a fixed price of $100,000. Since the signing of the contract inflation has advanced markedly, and the price of materials such as lumber, wiring, and plumbing has advanced at an even more rapid rate. Builder has completed one-half of the house when Speculator, short of funds because of rising interest rates, is compelled to order him to stop work. At the time work is stopped, it would cost an additional $70,000 to complete the house, and the going rate for the construction of a house of this type has advanced to $140,000. Builder sues Speculator (or her representative in bankruptcy, if you prefer a greater degree of realism).

To the nonlawyer it might come as a surprise to learn that the standard textbook treatment of Builder's claim would allow him to sue for $70,000 and not just for the $50,000 that represents one-half of the agreed price.[3] Yet the principle behind the clear intuition that Customer can get his money back in full in case I, if extended to case II, leads to just this result. This is the restitutionary principle, introduced in chapter 2, which holds that one who has been unjustly enriched at another's expense may not keep, should be forced to disgorge, the benefit he has received. If I intend to pay Mary ten dollars I owe her but send the money to you by mistake, you have been enriched at my expense and there is no reason why you should be allowed to keep that money. Similarly, if you steal the ten dollars from me you must return it. Well, if you have obtained ten dollars

from me on the faith of a promise that you are later unable or unwilling to keep, it seems equally unjust that you should keep the
money. Having repudiated your promise you cannot insist that my
obligations to you be judged according to my reciprocal promise.
The deal is off.

The logic of this argument extends to case II, for there is no reason
to limit it to the recovery of payments of money. Two collectors
agree to exchange antique watches. The first hands over his watch,
but the second collector is unable to deliver. It seem as fair that the
second collector return the watch as it does that Dealer in case I
return the money.[4] And if I gave the promise-breaker something
that he cannot return — I gave him a bottle of wine, which has been
drunk, or I have built him a part of a house on his land — surely the
restitutionary principle should still hold. Where return of the
specific good is impossible, the value of the benefit conferred should
be returned. And that is precisely what Builder urges in case II in
demanding not $50,000 but $70,000 — the value of the benefit he has
conferred.

We feel uncomfortable about the result in case II. Builder assumed the risk of price increases just as Speculator assumed the risk
of decreases, and the agreed price includes both parties' estimate of
these risks. Why should Builder now be able to shift onto Speculator
the burden of what has turned out to be a losing bargain? Because
Speculator broke the contract? But we have established that in enforcing his contract the victim of a breach is entitled only to his expectancy, to what he would have had if the contract had been completed. The point of contracting is to tie down the future, to allocate
the risks of a transaction between the two parties. But giving Builder
the choice between suing for his expectancy and suing for the actual
value of the benefit he has conferred seems to give him an unfair advantage. Speculator seems to bear the risk both of the house being
cheaper to build than estimated and of its being more expensive.
That cannot be the arrangement contracted for. There is an anomaly here, which needs explaining even in the face of our conviction
that in case I Customer should get his money back and thus be
relieved of a burden that under the deal he made would have been
his.[5] Consider this variant of case I:

III.    Owner has reason to believe there might be oil under his
land and engages Driller to sink an exploratory well. The cost of

the exploratory well is $100,000 paid in advance. After payment but before any drilling has taken place, exploratory wells drilled on neighboring land establish with virtual certainty that there are no oil deposits in the area. In the meantime, however, Driller has become involved in other, more lucrative operations and announces that he is unwilling to perform.

Should Driller be able to keep Owner's $100,000 on the ground that if Driller had performed his obligations it would have done Owner no good at all and he would have been out $100,000? Here we can see perhaps even more clearly the oddness of Driller's hiding behind a promise, which he did not even begin to keep, in order to limit Owner to the recovery of his expectation damages, that is, damages measured the contract.

By resisting restitution, Dealer, Railway Express, and Driller treat their opposite numbers (Customer, Stove Company, Owner) not as if they had made contracts to buy a car, deliver goods, or drill a well, but as if they had purchased options to demand these performances. Suppose for a moment that in case III Owner had purchased an option from Driller to call for the drilling of a well at a specified price or that in case I Customer had bought an option from Dealer on the gas guzzler. If Owner and Customer allowed their options to lapse when (as the hypotheticals posit) the deals proved unattractive, then of course they would lose the price of the options to Driller and Dealer. Option contracts are contracts to enter into contracts. An optionholder may convert his option into a straightforward contract, but he has the right not to go ahead with the transaction, has the right not to exercise his option. It is a preliminary, tentative, kind of arrangement.[6] Someone who buys an option seeks to do just that: to "keep his options open." This stands in contrast to someone who has made a deal. That person no longer keeps his options open, but now has committed himself. That is why the option concept hardly describes cases I and III.

The transaction in both cases looks to performance, and the price paid is the full price for performance. If Driller can refuse to perform and still keep the money, he reaps the full benefits of the decline in value of his own performance. In the allocation of risk contemplated by the contracts, Dealer lost the chance to sell his car more dearly to another customer, or took the chance that the cost to him of the cars might go up, and Driller assumed the risk that the cost of his performing the services might be dearer than he had expected, while Customer assumed the risk that the value of the car would go down and Owner took the risk that the hole would be dry. Dealer and Driller were compensated for taking these risks by being able to count on a fixed price for their goods and services. Customer and Owner were compensated for their risk by being assured of the goods and services at the particular price. If Dealer now gets to keep $2,000 without having delivered a car and Driller gets to keep $100,000 without having expended any resources in drilling, then the balance in the exchange has been altered. Viewed ex ante such a possibility increases the expected overall value of the contract to Dealer or Driller. Had Customer or Owner known ex ante about this possible improvement in the outcome for their opposite parties, they would have sought in the bargain to capture some portion of it, since the funds producing this incremental improvement in the expected value of the bargain to Dealer or Driller are provided by them. After the event the contract breakers can argue that their victims are no worse off than they would have been had the contract been performed. But this argument for damages rather than restitution seems plausible only *after* the event.

A contractual regime must maintain the integrity of bargains, and this means not reversing the allocation of risks on which the parties evaluated their bargain when they made them. Bargains are struck and their prices evaluated on the assumption that they will be kept. If they are not kept, the injured party may claim expectation damages. Contractual parties do not imagine that they will have to pay for performanances that they do not receive. Parties bind themselves reciprocally. If one party treats himself as not bound, the other may also treat himself as not bound. By breaking his contract, a contractual partner not only opens himself up to claims for damages but releases his opposite number.*

Thus Holmes's celebrated dictum that one always has the "option" to break a contract and that the sole consequence a contract-breaker need fear is a suit for damages goes too far, is too simple. The only *contractual* liability he incurs is indeed the liability to pay

---

*Professor Atiyah writes that until well into the eighteenth century contractual obligations were regularly treated as independent, so that the victim of even a total breach was obligated to render his counterperformance and had to rest content with a damage remedy alone. See Patrick Atiyah, *The Rise and Fall of Freedom of Contract* 208-216, 424 (Oxford, 1979). This cannot have been more than a presumption, however, since courts were quite familiar with the concept of conditional obligation. See A. W. B. Simpson, "*The Horwitz Thesis and the History of Contracts*," 46 *U. Chi. L. Rev.* 533, 544 (1979).

damages,[7] but this does not mean that there are no other consequences of his breach. The most important additional consequence is the possible release of his contractual partner from his obligation. Where there has been a prepayment or other performance on the faith of the contract, this release entails an obligation to effect restitution. In case II Speculator must make restitution to Builder for benefits conferred, and that means paying the $70,000 that Builder's work is worth. This does not in any way contradict the principle of contract as promise: Speculator, having breached, cannot appeal to that principle to limit her liability to pay the fair value of what she received. Any other outcome would disturb the expectations on which contractual terms are usually established. Moreover, the promissory principle is in no way undermined by seeing that obligation as released, for the reciprocity that was assumed in its formation has been violated.

## CONDITIONS

The importance of not being in the wrong carries one step further. Imagine that in cases I and III there had been no prepayment by the injured party. We have been inveighing against the presumptuousness of the contract-breaker's hiding behind a contract that he himself has broken so that he may retain a prepayment or other benefit, while forcing the injured party to recover only his expectancy damages. How much more audacious it would be for the contract-breaker to use the contract he himself breaks as an *affirmative* ground in his suit for the price. Imagine Driller suing for the profit he would have made had he drilled the well, though he admits that it was he who refused to go forward. When Owner balks, citing Driller's own breach, Driller urges that the Owner should perform his contractual duties and if he wants he should sue for damages—and as we have seen in this particular case Owner has suffered no damages from the undrilled well. It would be anomalous indeed to require Driller to return the prepayment, while allowing him to bring suit for that payment in exactly the same circumstances of breach. That Driller must fail in this suit follows a fortiori from our earlier determination that he must repay the price if he received it in prepayment.

The factor of not being in the wrong has played a large role in the thinking of the courts. Consider the leading cases of *Norrington v.*

*Wright*[8] and *Filley v. Pope.*[9] In both cases, American dealers were buying up used rails wherever they could find them to meet a speculative surge in demand. A sudden drop in the American market left dealers with commitments to buy rails at high prices, when they could expect to resell them for only fractions of those prices. In *Norrington*, the American's contract provided for monthly deliveries in specified minimum and maximum amounts. After two months of shipments, it appeared that the sellers were not complying with these schedules—sometimes going over and sometimes under. The buyers took this as a pretext for treating the sellers as being in "total breach" and refusing to accept or pay for any of the rails. In *Filley* the buyer's contention was even more extreme. There the contract called for shipment of rails to American ports from Glasgow. No vessels being available in Glasgow, the sellers loaded and shipped from the east coast of Scotland, this being a speedier way to procure delivery than if they had complied strictly with the terms of the contract. Once again the buyers used this divergence as a pretext for treating the contract as breached, and thus for refusing to accept or pay for the rails. This strategy was immensely advantageous to the buyers, disastrous to the sellers. If the buyers had been held to their contracts and remitted to a remedy in damages for the seller's deviations from the details of their undertakings, the buyers would have borne the whole burden of the fall in the market themselves: In neither of the two cases is there any reason to believe that the deviation from those strict terms had in fact caused significant damage.*

Astonishingly, in both cases the court held for the buyers on the argument that a contractual party is not required to pay for what he did not buy. As a general principle this makes sound sense, and indeed it follows from the principle developed out of cases I and III. Certainly if the sellers had delivered no rails at all, it would be outrageous to allow them to sue buyers for the price of the rails, leaving buyers to counterclaim for the damages they suffered by their nondelivery. This would force the buyers to suffer and pay over to the sellers the market loss they (the buyers) would have suf-

---

*In *Norrington* the deviation from the schedule was largely in the regularity of the shipments—that is, though some rails arrived earlier than the schedule required, others arrived later. This might have made it somewhat more difficult to dispose of the rails and in some instances might have meant that rails scheduled for earlier delivery had to be disposed of later when the market had fallen still further, but these losses were obviously trivial compared to the losses the buyer would have suffered as a result of the fall in the market if the contract had been strictly complied with and he had been forced to take delivery.

fered had the contract been strictly fulfilled. And even though the sellers delivered *something*, this should not be allowed to impose those losses on the buyers which the buyers would have suffered if the contract had been strictly performed. If, for instance, only one small shipment of rails consisting of a tiny fraction of the full contract amount had been made, this should make no difference to the result. If I contract to buy a specific good, you cannot deliver something quite different and force me to pay the contract price minus any damages I might suffer. This would in effect compel me to buy something I did not want, while leaving me with the contract losses I would have suffered if I had received what I had intended to buy. So it is not the principle that goes awry in *Norrington* and *Filley*, but its application.

The doctrine of substantial performance would preclude the outrageous result of these two cases while preserving intact the principle for which I have been arguing. Substantial performance seeks to accommodate the principle that the victim of a breach need not be held to his promise, need not pay when all he has received is a broken promise, while avoiding the absurdities of *Norrington* and *Filley*. If the contract-breaker has performed in large measure, to a substantial degree, by keeping the contract in force and requiring the victim to seek compensation for any deficiencies through the normal channels of contract recovery,[10] the victim is not being asked to pay for something he has not bought. And how much performance is substantial performance? When may someone sell a part perormance, receiving the whole price minus damages? Large differences may turn on small nuances here. There is a sharp discontinuity in result between the cases in which the victim of a breach of contract must cleave to the contract and seek his remedy solely within its terms and the cases in which he may ignore the contract altogether, either escaping his obligation to make a counterperformance (as in *Norrington*) or recovering restitution (as in cases I–III.) This reflects the sharp discontinuity between entering into contractual relations—assuming an obligation voluntarily—and not crossing that threshold.

The problem of substantial performance and the importance of not being in the wrong may be seen as aspects of the sometimes mysteriouos topic of conditions, which has already been touched on in chapter 4. Where a term of an agreement is treated as a condition, the result for the party on the losing end of that designation can be sharp and harsh.[11] For instance, beneficiaries of insurance policies have lost every penny of their claims by failing to comply with conditions of notice;[12] holders of options have lost lucrative opportunities by being a day or even an hour late in exercising their options.[13] And then there is *Clark v. West*:[14] A scholar had agreed with a publisher to write a treatise on the law of corporations, the contract providing that the author would be paid at the rate of $2 a page, but that he would receive an additional $4 a page on the condition that he abstain from alcohol during the period of his labors. Clark produced a fine treatise, but did take the occasional drink, so the publishers sought to pay only at the lower rate. (As I show later, justice triumphed and Clark recovered the full amount.)

Contractual obligation is based on promise, and promissory obligations are obligations freely undertaken. There is a threhold the obligor must willingly cross. He should be free of obligations he has not undertaken, and one way he can spell out the limit of his undertaking is just by stating how far he will be obliged—for example, I promise to pay "a reasonable price" for improvements to my house but no more than $5000. A promisor may also limit his obligation by making it conditional—for example, I promise to buy a particular car at a specified price, *unless* prior to the date of delivery gasoline rationing is instituted. The noninstitution of gasoline rationing is a condition of the obligation. If your promise is conditional, then unless the condition is met you are under no obligation. When the condition fails, the promisee has no obligation to enforce—he cannot, for instance, enforce your obligation, proposing to deduct whatever damage you have suffered. There just is no obligation. It is gone. And if the person with a conditional obligation happened to make prepayment, then the principles discussed above would allow him to obtain restitution of that prepayment, since that prepayment was given pursuant to an obligation that no longer exists.

The doctrine of substantial performance is a refinement of this concept of conditional obligation. The promise that Customer makes in case I or Owner makes in III is indeed conditional: If and when you deliver a car to me I will be obligated for the price; if and when you drill for me I will become obligated to pay. I am obligated to pay for the car, for the drilling, as you are obligated to deliver the car, to drill the well; but if you do not do your part my obligation to you lapses. But just as we have seen that some slight beginning of

performance will not be enough to activate the promisor's performance, so substantial performance—the rendering of all but a slight
proportion of the agreed-upon return—will establish that obligation. Delivery of a hubcap is not enough to establish the customer's
obligation to pay for a car in case I; delivery of all *but* a hubcap will
not prevent that obligation from coming into being. If the opposite
party has performed substantially, the obligor is not released; he
must fulfill his commitments and look to a damage remedy for
satisfaction in respect to his losses. He has crossed the threshold; the
opposite party's substantial performance keeps him across this
threshold; the less than substantial default does not put the obligor
back across the threshold into a domain of no commitment. The
obligor must calculate his remedies from within, not from without,
the contractual situation.

The courts in *Norrington* and *Filley* reached absurd results by
assuming that the schedule and departure terms respectively were
conditions.[15] They assumed this because they assumed that *every*
term was a condition. They assumed that every term was a condition on the fallacious reasoning that since it was their duty to respect
the autonomy of the parties and not to impose obligations upon
them that they had not assumed, therefore they must condition *all* of
the buyers' duties to the sellers on the strict compliance by the sellers
with *all* of the buyers' terms. But this begs the question. If the buyers
and sellers did not intend to treat minor, nonmaterial deviations
from the terms of the contract as conditions, it frustrates rather than
realizes the will of the parties for the courts to treat them as conditions. That the parties took all the terms of their contracts seriously
does not preclude giving such nonmaterial terms quite adequate effect by a damage remedy alone. Treating all terms as conditions
deprives bargainers of an important method for nuancing the allocations of risks. The sellers of the iron rails certainly did not imagine
that their departure in these trivial ways would release the buyers
from all obligations, and if the contract did not say so specifically why
should this unreasonable interpretation hold? One suspects that the
court felt some inhibition about judging that some terms are so important that they naturally stand as conditions while others are sufficiently marginal that they do not. But such exercises of judgment
are inevitable, and those courts whick seek to avoid them are guilty
of the same fallacy as their realist critics, in that they all (critic and
criticized) imagine that, since such exercises of judgment are neither

mechanical nor beyond controversy, making them is therefore a nonneutral, political act imposed upon the parties and not one implementing their wills.[16]

This analysis implies that had the parties specifically so provided, every trivial departure from the contractual arrangement would have to be treated as a breach of condition and thus a release from obligation. Is this shocking? Must we accept this conclusion? If the parties had really agreed to such a provision, the decisions would be more acceptable. In most situations we may suspect that they have not; one of the parties has laid a subtle trap so that such a consequence comes as a surprise to the other. The concepts discussed in chapter 6 are sufficient to block this bad faith maneuver. If it is not a surprise, but rather a freely accepted gamble, there are still ways to mitigate the rigors of that result and to avoid forfeitures in many cases. These mitigating doctrines are the subject of the next section.[17]

## WAIVERS, FORFEITURES, REPUDIATIONS

Consider this case:

> IV.  Builder undertakes to build a house to have certain specifications for completion by a certain date. He does not complete it in time and there are slight departures from plan (for instance, a different but equivalent brand of waste pipe is used). Owner claims that since the specifications and the completion time were expressly denominated conditions, he is released from his obligation and may keep the house without paying for it.[18]

Owner's suggestion is absurd. The doctrine of conditions does not necessarily force such a forfeiture upon Builder. Imagine this variant of such harsh cases as *Norrington* and *Filley:* The buyer specifically provides that the size and schedule of shipments and the port of departure are conditions, and that failure to comply would release him. Even in such a case the buyer must either reject the iron rails when they arrive or—if he keeps them—must pay for them. Nothing in the doctrine of conditions suggests that the buyer may keep the rails, while being released from his obligation to pay. This obvious point may be explicated in two ways. First, we may say that since the buyer inserted the condition for his own benefit, he need not avail himself of it. In the language of the law, he may "waive" the condition. Second, there is simply nothing in the doctrine of conditions I have been elaborating that suggests that the buyer's option to claim release is also an option to claim the full benefit of the bargain without any of its obligations. There would indeed be a forfeiture if the seller had to hand over his goods without getting paid.*

It is consistent with the theory of conditions that the beneficiary of a condition, here the buyer, is not bound to avail himself of it; he may waive it. If the seller ships the goods from the east coast of Scotland rather than Glasgow in a rising market, the buyer may choose to accept. If the breach of a condition automatically released the parties, not just at the option of the one imposing the condition, then the party subject to the condition could escape obligations that had become unfavorable simply by breaching the condition. And so we see that the doctrine of conditions implies that the condition-holder must be able to waive the breach of condition if he chooses. Further, he may choose to waive the breach of condition *as a condition*, while continuing to treat it as a breach of a nonfundamental term and suing for damages.**[19] None of this harshness involves a forfeiture—at least not a forfeiture in the sense that the seller has parted with goods without getting paid for them. He has forfeited his rights under the contract, to be sure, but he is released from its duties as well.

What then, of case IV? How do we prevent Builder in that case from suffering a forfeiture, while still giving force to the doctrine of conditions and respecting the privileges Owner built into his contract? The case seems difficult, but only because of the special facts,

---

*I do not wish to minimise the hardship of the doctrine as it remains: If a buyer does avail himself of a condition, he can shift the whole burden of a declining market to the seller. But that is a risk which the buyer and seller ex hypothesi knowingly assumed. Presumably the prices charged reflected this risk. After all, the seller might also have sold the buyer an option to buy, which the buyer would be free to exercise or not as he chose—thus once again forcing upon the seller the risk of a falling market, a risk for which the seller presumably could have demanded compensation.

**Because of the harsh effect of conditions, courts will be astute to find a waiver—even if it means stretching a point. Moreover, even courts firmly wedded to the formalities of consideration in respect to the modification or discharge of contracts (see chapter 3 supra) do not require consideration for an effective waiver. So in *Clark v. West* the fact that the publisher knew that Clark took a drink from time to time and yet accepted the manuscript without comment, might constitute an implicit waiver—particularly since the point of the arrangement was to get a satisfactory manuscript, which publisher did. As the court put it, the idea was that Clark stay sober to write, not that he write to stay sober. The publisher's whole course of conduct indicated that it got what it had bargained for and so could not insist on the condition.

not because of some flaw in the theory. As we saw in respect to movable goods, if the condition-holder chooses to retain the goods he must pay for them. So in case IV the same point holds. If Owner retains the benefit under the contract, then he must pay for it. This is just another application of the restitution principle. True, the breach of condition has released him from his contractual obligations, but it has not released him from the quite different obligation to pay for tangible benefits that he chooses to retain. But how can you return a half-built house? Of course you cannot, which is only to say that you cannot fully avail yourself of the benefit of the condition in your favor. The best use you can make of that condition is to refuse to pay *in contract terms* for the benefit conferred, but rather to offer to pay no more than the fair value. After all the basis of the payment is no longer the contract but the principle of restitution. And if the fair value is less than the contract price, this distinction will have some bite.

There are further subtleties arising from the interplay of the restitutionary and the promissory principles. If in a case like II Builder completed the house down to the last doorknob and Speculator refused to pay, Builder could not claim "restitution" for the value of the benefit he had conferred, but rather would be limited to a suit for the price in the agreement.*[20] Or there is the

*The result is a painful anomaly: By breaching later, when she has received more and Builder has performed substantially, Speculator may be in a better situation than if she had breached when the house was only half built. If the contract is advantageous to her she need only pay the contract price when she is in possession of the *whole* benefit, but must pay the value of what she had received — perhaps far in excess of the contract price — if she repudiates after receiving part. See not 3 supra. At this point my powers of rationalization give out. The *Restatement* (2d), tent. draft no. 14, sec. 387 (2) proposed to cut this Gordian knot by providing that "the injured party cannot recover a larger sum as restitution on performance of part of his duties than he would have recovered on full performance." This proposal was, however, subsequently withdrawn by the Reporter, Professor Allan Farnsworth, who stated: "The authorities, Palmer says [*Restitution*, supra note 2], heavily favor the rule that you can exceed the contract price. My reading of the authorities is that there are very few cases in which this arises, and that you can find enough authority either way to permit the Institute to go either way . . . What I think we could say is that courts have recognized that the contract price is evidence of the benefit to the party in breach, and therefore very rarely allowed the claimant to get more than the contract price. That is a completely accurate statement of the law. It does not, I think, tell the reader which way a court will go. My feeling is that it would be prudent if the Institute left that one open." American Law Institute, *Proceedings — 56th Annual Meeting, 1979* 405-408 (Philadelphia, 1980). The new provision, minus the proposal, appears now as section 373.

Paradox breaks out in the sale of goods as well. A buyer may recover a prepayment for wrongfully undelivered goods even when their value has declined below that amount, UCC § 2-711(1), but the seller can recover only the contract price for accepted goods, however much their market value may have increased, UCC § 2-709(1)(a).

problem arising in cases like II where the party who has partly performed (Builder) is in breach and cannot or will not complete his
performance. Builder is in a bind: He cannot sue Speculator for
breach of contract, since Speculator has not breached—Builder
has—and it would be preposterous to allow Builder to sue for his
own breach. It is equally awkward for Builder to sue for restitution
of the value of the benefit he has conferred, since Speculator can
reasonably point to the contract as spelling out the only terms on
which she consented to receive these benefits.[21] In contrast to case
II, we do not in this case have the party who resists restitution hiding
behind a contract she has herself broken. On the contrary,
Speculator in this case defends against Builder's restitutionary claim
just by invoking a contract that she has never broken. (Case V in
chapter 2 is another illustration of this problem.)

What we see is an alternation in the priority between the restitutionary and the promissory principles. The restitutionary principle
is more primitive, closer to what justice in general requires in dealings between unconnected strangers. By making promises, strangers
may supplant that primitive regime with a voluntary regime of their
own making. Yet he who would urge such a supplanting regime had
better be in a position to do so. He is not in a position to do so if his
dues in the more refined promissory club are not close to being paid
up. In other words, he cannot resist being judged by the more
primitive standards of restitutionary justice if he has violated the
basic premises of the supplanting regime, if he is not in substantial
compliance with his contractual obligations. This was the lesson of
cases I-III. The complementary principle bars Builder in the variant
of case II just posed. He cannot urge the restitutionary regime
against Speculator, when Speculator has complied in all respects
with a contract the parties made about this very subject matter.
They freely engaged to govern their relations by a voluntary regime
of their own choosing. Speculator is willing, and so she may insist.

In the end, the law will swing back another beat. For Builder to
be deprived of both a restitutionary and a promissory remedy works
a forfeiture on him—and gives Speculator a windfall. A practical
solution—the one that now generally obtains—gives Builder a
restitutionary remedy for the benefits he has conferred on
Speculator, but limited by the contract price as a ceiling. So if in
case II Builder had defaulted after having built one-half of a house
with a completed value of $140,000 and a contract price of $100,000,

he could recover not $70,000 but $50,000.[22] To allow him more would permit him to use his own breach as a way of improving his situation over what it would have been had he kept his word. To allow Builder to profit at Speculator's expense by breaking his promise is inconsistent with the judgment that breaking his promise is wrong. At the same time, to allow Builder no remedy—to subject him to a forfeiture—is inconsistent with the principle that all an injured party is entitled to is the value of his expectancy.*

The doctrine of conditions gives great importance to not being in the wrong. The party in the wrong has a lot to lose. Inevitably this gives rise to some elaborate jockeying for position.[23] Someone subject to a contract that looks as if it is going to end up unfavorably for him (like the buyers in *Norrington* and *Filley*) will have every reason to look for defaults on his partner's part that could be characterized as breaches of condition and thus would release him from an onerous obligation. And the party who has the more favorable side of the deal must be exceedingly careful to comply with every demand, lest he be subject to the claim of a breach of condition and thus lose his advantageous bargain. This maneuvering becomes downright comical in the case where the party claiming the benefit of the release by virtue of a breach of condition would himself have been unwilling or perhaps even unable to perform. Such a party must hope that the other party will breach before he does and thus bear the whole burden of the loss.

Consider yet another variant on *Norrington* or *Filley*. Assume a contract by which buyer's prompt payment is also made a condition of the contract, such that in a rising market sellers could have suspended their further performance in the event of a delay in payment. Now what if a seller guilty of a breach of condition in a *falling* market could prove that the buyer could not have paid for the goods if they had been shipped in time or from the right port?[24] Should this somehow deprive the buyer of the right to avail himself of the conditions that favor him? I don't see why. Indeed, I don't see why even if the buyer had actually been in default first he should for that reason automatically lose the right to avail himself of *his* conditions. The

*Of course Speculator may herself sue for damages caused by Builder's wrongful refusal to complete his contract. It will presumably cost her $70,000 to get someone else to finish the house. The extra $20,000 she can recover from Builder, subtracting it from what she pays him. At the end of the day she will have her house and will have paid $100,000 for it—just as she expected. I disregard her legal expenses.

significance of a condition is that it gives an option to effect a release from obligation: Even if the buyer had been in default on his payments so that the seller *might have* released himself from his obligations, still, unless the seller had in fact so released himself, the contract would continue in force on its original terms (with seller having a right to damages—in this case interest on the late payments). Since the contract is still in effect, the buyer is now in a position to demand compliance with *his* conditions.

An inducement to scramble is particularly acute in one rather special situation:

> V.   On January 2 Brenda contracts with Arthur that he work for her beginning July 1. On March 1 she wrongfully tells him that she has hired somebody else and that the job will not be available. On June 15 Arthur takes another, lower-paying job in some distant place to which he removes. On July 1 Brenda writes Arthur stating that since he has not presented himself for work under their agreement she considers herself released from all obligation. Arthur would nonetheless like to sue for the difference between the wages he is receiving and the higher wages promised in the contract with Brenda.[25]

Brenda's claim will be that Arthur's working for her was the condition of any obligation that she might have, and that since he has disabled himself from fulfilling this condition, she is released and cannot be sued. The suggestion is obviously outrageous. What blocks it? Common sense suggests that Brenda cannot insist on the performance of a condition when she herself is in default and Arthur has not waived his rights arising from her breach. Once again we see the importance of not being in the wrong—and Brenda is clearly in the wrong. But what if Brenda says she is *not* in the wrong? What if she says she was perfectly prepared to take on Arthur on July 1, which is all the contract required her to do? Brenda says she is not in breach because her obligations only arose on July 1, at which date she was fully ready to perform. If her answer were allowed to stand, an obvious injustice would result. What is it and how is it to be avoided?

One device is to say that in fact Brenda's obligations do not begin on July 1 but arise with the making of the contract. These earlier obligations are said to be obligations of cooperation, noninterference, and the like.[26] Her statement of March 1 is a breach of these obligations to act with loyalty to her undertaking from the moment of its formation. If such a breach is also a breach of condition, Arthur is excused from his obligations and may also bring suit for his damages. A less forced way to get at the felt injustice of Brenda's claim is to say that Brenda, having announced her intention to breach on March 1, cannot complain if Arthur takes her at her word.[27] That certainly is how we feel about the matter, but the response does seem a little too perfunctory to stand as an explanation.

The purpose of contractural obligation is to provide assurances into the future. Brenda has done that on January 2. Her declaration of March 1 contradicts this assurance. Can Arthur be blamed if he does not ignore Brenda's repudiation? It is after all more useful for him to set about finding alternative employment immediately. Waiting until July 1 might mean missing splendid opportunities, and although Brenda will eventually have to respond in damages, what is gained if he does forgo an earlier alternative? So utility is on the side of allowing Arthur to take Brenda at her word. But is it fair? Brenda, after all, might say that she might have changed her mind at any time — as in fact she eventually did. The simplest answer is the best. Arthur is entitled to rely on Brenda's word given in the contract of January 2. On March 1 she says something meaning Arthur no longer to expect that she will fulfill her promise. It would be unfair to Arthur to penalize him for seeking to protect his interests in the face of her threat. If you create an expectation intending another person to act upon it, it is a kind of entrapment then to claim that the other person's acting as you meant him to act constitutes a violation of *your* rights. You are not estopped if you do something you have a perfect right to do — for example, leaving your window open in the summer, even if you have reason to believe that somebody might take advantage of this to burglarize your house. (At least you are not estopped against the burglar.) But Brenda has not done something within her rights or something neutral, such as leaving a window open; she has threatened to act in violation of her obligations to Arthur. She has done so meaning him no longer to expect that she will fulfill her obligations. The entrapment lies in her then blaming Arthur for protecting himself against this wrongful threat. Arthur's failure to show up at Brenda's on July 1, his failure to comply with what may have been a condition in the January 1 contract, therefore will not under these circumstances foreclose him from claiming any of the rights he may have.

In holding Brenda to her repudiation we once again, as in the case of waiver, allow the extinction of a contractual right by a voluntary act that is inconsistent with the assertion of that right and that undermines the actor's moral title to insist on the promise. We say that Brenda's bad faith maneuvers estop her from enforcing the contract, and estoppel like waiver is a nonpromissory act that weakens or extinguishes promissory rights.

But what if on February 29, unknown to Brenda, Arthur had already agreed with Charlotte to start work on June 15? In that circumstance he could hardly say that his beginning work for Charlotte on June 15 was a *response* to Brenda's repudiation. Could he still sue Brenda for the difference between the wages Brenda would have paid him and the wages he is earning from Charlotte? Note that if he had *announced* to Brenda his disloyal plans when he made them on February 29, then it would be Brenda who could do the suing—perhaps recovering the difference between the salary she had promised Arthur and the salary she must now pay to David, who will take his place. If Arthur had merely discussed alternative employment with Charlotte, had reached no agreement but in his heart had concluded that he would break his contract, it seems pretty clear that it would still be Brenda who is in the wrong, who repudiates, and who must pay. Otherwise the inquiry into motives would be too delicate indeed. But how can a circumstance of which Brenda does not know—the circumstance that Arthur has in fact concluded an arrangement with Charlotte on February 29—operate to release Brenda from her obligation or at least to turn what would otherwise have been her wrongful repudiation on March 1 into no repudiation at all? Is it because Arthur is no longer prejudiced by what Brenda says to him on March 1? Brenda intends to prejudice him but she does not succeed. Notice that this is different from the situation where Arthur is determined in his heart to work for Charlotte but has made no engagement to that effect, for in that case he is still free (in the sense of free from an obligation to Charlotte) to fulfill his obligations to Brenda, and for all we know he may yet change his mind and decide to do so. So the circumstances are complex, each step along the way is fair and reasonable, and the combination of steps is not unfair. It does show, however, that in such a circumstance it is important not only not to be in the wrong but not to be in the wrong first.

These doctrines of waiver, repudiation, and estoppel are a response to the significant power a contract gives the promisee over a promisor; a promise may call for sacrifices far in excess of what residual, background nonpromissory principles of fairness and decency require. That is why a promisee may not trifle with what he has. This is shown again at a later stage of the relationship, after there has clearly been a breach. If the victim of a breach can protect himself from its consequences he must do so. He has a duty to mitigate damages.[28] (Arthur, for instance, mitigates the damages from Brenda's anticipatory repudiation by looking for other work.) The duty to mitigate does go further than waiver or estoppel in one sense, however: The contract right is diminished not because the rightholder acted inconsistently with it but because he failed to take some further action, further action that in fact benefits the contract-breaker by reducing his potential liability. This is a duty, a kind of altruistic duty, toward one's contractual partner, the more altruistic that it is directed to a partner in the wrong. But it is a duty without cost, since the victim of the breach is never worse off for having mitigated. Rather it is a duty that recognizes that contractual liabilities are onerous enough that they should not be needlessly exacerbated. And if the victim of a breach fails in his duty the only penalty he suffers is the proportional loss of his own remedial rights.*

This series of alternations in and out of the promise principle has a disquietingly binary look about it, just as the doctrine of conditions has a disquieting abruptness. If all conditions were demoted to the status of mere contractual terms, for the breach of which only

*The rarely encountered doctrine of condonation—better known in divorce law—carries this idea one step further and joins it to the principle of waiver and estoppel. In one case, In re Nagel, 278 F. 105 (2d Cir. 1921), an employer learned that his employee had been disloyal in a way that would have justified discharging him. The employer neither said nor did anything about this breach for several months, and then when he needed to reduce his work force used the breach as a ground for discharge. This was found to be improper. Why? My sense is that the court did not wish to give the employer an axe to hold over the employee's head indefinitely; either the employer must discharge the employee promptly or he reinstates the relation on its former terms.

Another combination of estoppel and mitigation notions is exemplified by the Uniform Commercial Code's rule that the victim of a breach must give notice to its perpetrator, thus providing an opportunity for cure or perhaps negotiation and accommodation. U.C.C. §2-607(3). See also Cummings v. Connecticut General Life Insurance Company, 102 Vt. 351, 148 A. 484 (1930). But cf. Cawley v. Weiner, 236 N.Y. 357, 140 N.E. 724 (1923).

damages could be recovered, the whole range between full compliance, partial compliance, and no compliance would represent a
smooth continuum of modulating recoveries. As it is, however, there
are sharp discontinuities, and these are disturbing to the economic
or marginalist mentality. That mentality sees discontinuities as a
symptom of irrationality. What I have tried to show is that such
discontinuities are unavoidable, and indeed that they are a sign that
we are in the domain of right and wrong, which is a domain of
discontinuity. The utilitarian, believing right and wrong not to be
an autonomous domain but one under the hegemony of good and
bad, of better and worse, is committed to seeing all judgments as
judgments of degree. But if the domain of right and wrong is seen as
autonomous, it must contain sharp breaks: between the permissible
and the impermissible, between the obligatory and the optional.
And contractual obligation (promissory obligation) is obligation
after all. A particular act may be more or less good or indifferent,
but once it is the subject of a promise it is transformed and becomes
obligatory. This is a discrete step, and so it should be no surprise that
judgments (and consequences) visited upon acts will vary sharply
(discontinuously) depending on whether or not obligations may be
invoked in respect to those acts.

The back and forth between expectation and restitution, and between recovery and no recovery reflect the appropriateness or inap-
propriateness of a party's invoking another's obligations. Since the
terms of obligations are freely invented and imposed by the parties
on themselves, they may mold them as they wish. They may condition them, and if they do, their wishes must be respected. But other
circumstances switch the force of obligation on or off: the other party's failure to do his part, repudiation, a frustrating event, the fault
of both parties, the kind of advantage to be drawn from one's own or
from the other's fault. The law of contracts, just because it is rooted
in promise and so in right and wrong, is a ramifying system of moral
judgments working out the entailments of a few primitive principles—primitive principles that determine the terms on which free
men and women may stand apart from or combine with each other.
These are indeed the laws of freedom.[29]

NOTES

INDEX

# Notes

## 1. INTRODUCTION: THE LIFE OF CONTRACT

1. *A Treatise of Human Nature* 526 (Selby-Bigge ed. Oxford, 1888).

2. Compare Henry Sidgwick, *Elements of Politics*: "In a summary view of the civil order of society, as constituted by the individualistic ideal, performance of contract represents the chief *positive* element, protection of life and property being the chief *negative* element . . ." Quoted in Friedrich Kessler and Grant Gilmore, *Contracts* 4 (2d ed. Boston, 1970). This idea is expressed in Friedrich Hayek's reference to a "private sphere," *The Constitution of Liberty* 21 (Chicago, 1960) and Robert Nozick's description of violation of rights as "boundary crossing," *Anarchy, State and Utopia* 57 (New York, 1974). See also Duncan Kennedy, "The Structure of Blackstone's Commentaries," 28 *Buffalo L. Rev.* 205, 234 (1979).

3. Ronald Dworkin, *Taking Rights Seriously* chs. 4, 7, and app. at 294-330 (Cambridge, 1978); Robert Nozick, *Anarchy, State and Utopia* ix (New York, 1974); and John Rawls, *A Theory of Justice* §6 (Cambridge, 1971)

are the principal contemporary statements. See also Charles Fried, *Right and Wrong* ch. 4 (Cambridge, 1978).

4. See Patrick Atiyah, *The Rise and Fall of Freedom of Contract* 405-419 (Oxford, 1979); Kessler and Gilmore, supra note 2, at 1-14; Max Radin, "Contract Obligation and the Human Will," 43 *Colum. L. Rev.* 575 (1943).

5. Atiyah, supra note 4, pt. III.

6. Fried, review of Atiyah, 93 *Harv. L. Rev.* 1858, 1864-1865 (1980); Roscoe Pound, "Contract or Bargain," 33 *Tulane L. Rev.* 455 (1959).

7. Atiyah, supra note 4; Lawrence Friedman, *Contract Law in America* (Madison, 1965); Grant Gilmore, *The Death of Contract* (Columbus, 1974); Morton Horwitz, *The Transformation of American Law* ch. 6 (Cambridge, 1977); Duncan Kennedy, supra note 2, at 356, and "Form and Substance in Private Law Adjudication," 89 *Harv. L. Rev.* 1685 (1976); Anthony Kronman, "Contract Law and Distributive Justice," 89 *Yale L. J.* 472 (1980); Ian Macneil, "The Many Futures of Contracts," 47 *So. Cal. L. Rev.* 691 (1974).

8. Lon Fuller and William Perdue, "The Reliance Interest in Contract Damages," 46 *Yale L. J.* 52, 373 (1936, 1937).

9. Gilmore, supra note 7, at 87.

10. Emile Durkheim, *The Division of Labor in Society* ch. 7 (Simpson trans. New York, 1933); Karl Llewellyn, "What Price Contract: An Essay in Perspective," 40 *Yale L. J.* 704 (1931).

11. The locus classicus is Morris Cohen, "The Basis of Contract Law," 46 *Harv. L. Rev.* 553 (1933), whose view Kessler and Gilmore epitomize thus: "Distributive justice has replaced commutative justice." Supra note 2 at 11. Robert Hale, "Bargaining, Duress and Economic Liberty," 43 *Colum. L. Rev.* 603 (1943); Kennedy, supra note 7; Kronman, supra note 7.

12. *Economic Analysis of Law* chs. 3 and 4 (2d ed. Boston, 1977); "Utility, Economics, and Legal Theory," 8 *J. Legal Stud.* 103 (1979).

## 2: CONTRACT AS PROMISE

1. On the right and the good the critical discussion is John Rawls, *A Theory of Justice* §§68, 83-85 (Cambridge, 1971), which harks back to Immanuel Kant, *Groundwork of the Metaphysics of Morals* (Paton trans., Harper Torchbooks ed. New York, 1964) where the contrast is made between the right and happiness. See also W. D. Ross, *The Right and the Good* (Oxford, 1930); Ronald Dworkin, "Liberalism," in *Public and Private Morality* (S. Hampshire ed. Cambridge, England, 1978). On the relation between liberalism and responsibility, see Friedrich Hayek, *The Constitution of Liberty* ch. 5 (Chicago, 1960); Charles Fried, *Right and Wrong* 124-126 (Cambridge, 1978); Rawls, supra at 519. For a different view see C. B. Macpherson, *The Political Theory of Possessive Individualism — Hobbes to Locke* (Oxford, 1962).

2. Immanuel Kant, *The Metaphysical Elements of Justice* 54-55 (Ladd trans. Indianapolis, 1965).

3. See Charles Fried, *An Anatomy of Values* 81-86 (Cambridge, 1970);

Henry Sidgwick, *Elements of Politics*, quoted in Friedrich Kessler and Grant Gilmore, *Contracts* 4 (2d ed. Boston, 1970).

4. Sissela Bok, *Lying: Moral Choice in Public Life* (New York, 1978); Fried, supra note 1, ch. 3.

5. This example is based on Adams v. Gillig, 199 N.Y. 314, 92 N.E. 670 (1930).

6. See generally Page Keeton, "Fraud: Statements of Intention," 15 *Texas L. Rev.* 185 (1937).

7. See generally Robert Goff and Gareth Jones, *The Law of Restitution* ch. 1 (2d. ed. London, 1978).

8. For a strong statement of the tort and benefit principles as foundations of contract law, see Patrick Atiyah, *The Rise and Fall of Freedom of Contract* 1-7 (Oxford, 1979). A remarkable article stating the several moral principles implicit in contract law is George Gardner, "An Inquiry into the Principles of the Law of Contracts," 46 *Harv. L. Rev.* 1 (1932).

9. For a review of Anglo-American writing on promise from Hobbes to modern times, see Atiyah, supra note 8, at 41-60, 649-659. There has been a lively debate on the bases for the moral obligation of promises in recent philosophical literature. Some philosophers have taken a line similar to that of Atiyah and Gilmore, deriving the obligation of promise from the element of reliance. The strongest statement is Neil MacCormick, "Voluntary Obligations and Normative Powers," *Proceedings of the Aristotelian Society*, supp. vol. 46, at 59 (1972). See also Pall Ardal, "And That's a Promise," 18 *Phil. Q.* 225 (1968); F. S. McNeilly, "Promises Demoralized," 81 *Phil. Rev.* 63 (1972). G. J. Warnock, *The Object of Morality* ch. 7 (London, 1971), offers an effective refutation along the lines in the text, but his affirmative case proposes that the obligation of a promise rests on the duty of veracity, the duty to make the facts correspond to the promise. For an excellent discussion of this last suggestion and a proposal that accords with my own, see Don Locke, "The Object of Morality and the Obligation to Keep a Promise," 2 *Canadian J. of Philosophy* 135 (1972). Locke's emphasis on trust seems a clearer and sounder version of H. A. Prichard's proposal that the obligation of a Promise rests on a more general "agreement to keep agreements." *Moral Obligation* ch. 7 (Oxford, 1957).

10. A number of the philosophers who disagree with the Atiyah-MacCormick argument emphasize the conventional aspect of the invocation of the promissory form, as well as the self-imposed nature of the obligation. E.g. Joseph Raz, "Voluntary Obligations," *Proceedings of the Aristotelian Society*, supp. vol. 46, at 79 (1972); Raz, "Promises and Obligations," in *Law, Morality and Society* (Hacker, Raz eds. Oxford, 1977); John Searle, *Speech Acts* 33-42, 175-188 (Cambridge, 1969); Searle, "What Is a Speech Act?" in *The Philosophy of Language* (John Searle ed. Oxford, 1971). The locus classicus of this view of promising is John Rawls, "Two Concepts of Rules," 64 *Phil. Rev.* 3 (1955). The general idea goes back, of course, to Ludwig Wittgenstein, *Philosophical Investigations* § 23. For Hume's account of the conventional nature of promissory obligation, see *A Treatise of Human Nature* 516-525 (Selby-Bigge ed Oxford, 1888).

11. Stanley Cavell's contention in *The Claim of Reason* 293-303 (Oxford, 1979) that promising is not a practice or an institution, because unlike the case of a game one cannot imagine setting it up or reforming it and because promising is not an office, seems to me beside the point. Kant's discussion, supra note 2, shows that morality can mandate that there be a convention with certain general features, as does Hume's discussion supra note 10, though Hume's morality is a more utilitarian one.

12. David Lewis, *Convention* (Cambridge, 1969).

13. Supra note 10.

14. Here I side with David Lyons, *The Forms and Limits of Utilitarianism* (Oxford, 1965) in a continuing debate. For the most recent statement of the contrary position, see Richard Brandt, *A Theory of the Good and Right* (Oxford, 1979). For an excellent introduction, see J. J. C. Smart and Bernard Williams, *Utilitarianism: For and Against* (Cambridge, England, 1973). I argue that it is a mistake to treat Rawls's discussion of promising in "Two Concepts of Rules," supra note 10, as an instance of rule-utilitarianism in my review of Atiyah, 93 *Harv. L. Rev.* 1863n18 (1980). See also Charles Landesman, "Promises and Practices," 75 *Mind* (n.s.) 239 (1966).

15. This was in fact Bentham's general perspective. See also Brandt, supra note 14.

16. Compare Rawls, supra note 1, ch. 6, where it is argued that (*a*) the deduction of the principles of justice for institutions, and (*b*) a showing that a particular institution is just are not sufficient to generate an obligation to comply with that institution. Further principles of natural duty and obligation must be established.

17. See Locke, supra note 9; Prichard, supra note 9; Raz, supra note 10.

18. American Law Institute, *Restatement (1st) of the Law of Contracts* [hereafter cited as *Restatement* (1st) or (2d)], § 329, Comment a: "In awarding compensatory damages, the effort is made to put the injured party in as good a position as that in which he would have been put by full performance of the contract . . ."; E. Allan Farnsworth, "Legal Remedies for Breach of Contract," 70 *Colum. L. Rev.* 1145 (1970); Gardner, supra note 8; Charles Goetz and Robert Scott, "Enforcing Promises: An Examination of the Basis of Contract," 80 *Yale L. J.* 1261 (1980).

19. See Fuller and Perdue, "The Reliance Interest in Contract Damages," 46 *Yale L. J.* 52, 373 (1936, 1937); Gardner, supra note 8.

20. For discussions of these issues see Fried, supra note 3, at 169-177; Rawls, supra note 1, §85; and the essays in *The Identities of Persons* (Amelie Rorty ed. Berkeley, 1976) and *Personal Identity* (John Perry ed. Berkeley, 1975).

21. See Atiyah, supra note 8, at 140-141 for a discussion of these early sources. See my review of Atiyah, 93 *Harv. L. Rev.* 1858, 1864-1865 (1980) for a further discussion of these and other early sources.

22. 227 Mo. App. 175, 51 S.W.2d 572 (1932).

23. *Restatement* (1st) §333(d).

24. Gardner, supra note 8, at 15, 22-23.

25. This is the problem that is standardly dealt with in contract texts under the rubric of consequential damages, or the principle in *Hadley v. Baxendale*

9 Exch. 341 (1854). See Gardner, supra note 8, at 28-30. Holmes, in Globe Refining Co. v. Landa Cotton Oil Co., 190 U.S. 540 (1903) explained the limitation of liability for consequential damages in terms of the agreement itself: The defendant is liable only for those risks he explicitly or tacitly agreed to assume. This conception has been generally rejected in favor of a vaguer standard by which defendant is liable for any risks of which he had "reason to know" at the time of the agreement. UCC §2-715 comment 2. Holmes's test seems more consonant with the thesis of this work. See Pothier, *The Law of Obligations*, quoted in Lon Fuller and Melvin Eisenberg, *Basic Contract Law* 27 (3rd ed. St. Paul, 1972). The difference between the two positions is not great: first, because it is always within the power of the parties to limit or expand liability for consequential damages by the agreement itself, UCC §2-719(3); second, because the "reason to know" standard means that the defendant at least has a fair opportunity to make such an explicit provision.

26. UCC §2-318; William Prosser, *Torts* ch. 17 (4th ed. St. Paul, 1971).

27. 133 N.W.2d 267, 26 Wis.2d 683 (1965).

28. See Stanley Henderson, "Promissory Estoppel and Traditional Contract Doctrine," 78 *Yale L. J.* 343, 357-360 (1969); see generally Friedrich Kessler and Edith Fine, *"Culpa in Contrahendo,* Bargaining in Good Faith, and Freedom of Contract: A Comparative Study," 77 *Harv. L. Rev.* 401 (1964).

29. *Nicomachean Ethics*, bk. V, iv-v.

30. See John Dawson, "Restitution or Damages?," 20 *Ohio St. L. J.* 175 (1959); Gardner, supra note 8, at 18-27. For a fuller discussion of restitution and contracts see chapter 8 infra.

31. Goff and Jones, supra note 7, at 69; the problem raised in the footnote is treated at 88-89.

32. Britton v. Turner, 6 N.H. 281 (1834).


## 3. CONSIDERATION

1. *Restatement* (1st) §19. The definition of consideration is as follows: (1) something of value must have been given in exchange for the promise to be enforced [see *Restatement* (1st) §75(1), *Restatement* (2d) §17(1)]; (2) with manifestation of mutual assent of the parties to make such an exchange (the "bargaining for" requirement) [*Restatement* (1st) §75(1), *Restatement* (2d) §71(1-2)].

2. The common law rule is that consideration is not required for enforcement of a promise under seal. See *Restatement* (1st) §110; *Restatement* (2d) §95 (1); 1 Samuel Williston, *Contracts* (3rd ed. Walter Jaeger, Mt. Kisco, 1957) (hereafter cited as Williston with volume numer) §217; 1 Arthur Corbin, *Contracts* §252 (St. Paul, 1963) (hereafter cited as Corbin with volume number). This is, however, a matter that has been the subject of extensive legislative action. See 1 Williston §219A, 1 Corbin §254, and *Restatement* (2d) §95, tent. draft no. 1-7, ch. 4, at 189 for a summary of the state of the law. Roughly half the states still recognize the seal, though many in a

weakened form; the effect of a seal may range from a complete substitute for consideration to a substantive though rebuttable presumption of consideration, to an allocation of pleading requirements and burdens of proof on the issue, to mere allocation of the issue to judge or jury. The other half of the states and UCC §2-203 have explicitly abolished the effect of the seal altogether.

3. UCC §2-205 removes the requirement of consideration for a promise to hold open an offer to buy or sell goods, but limits the period of irrevocability to three months and requires a writing separately signed by the promisor. See N.Y. Gen. Oblig. Law §5-1109 for a similar but more general provision.

4. 1 Williston §120, notes 7-9, for a summary.

5. E.g. UCC §2-209; N.Y. Gen. Oblig. Law §5-1103.

6. E.g. Cal. Civ. Code §1606; Ga. Code Ann. §20-303.

7. See Melvin Eisenberg, "Donative Promises," 47 *U. Chi. L. Rev.* 1, 2-7 (1980), for an excellent discussion and review of the authorities; see also Charles Goetz and Robert Scott, "Enforcing Promises: An Examination of the Basis of Contract," 89 *Yale L. J.* 1261, at 1261-1262 (1980). The neglect of donative promises is noted with regret by Roscoe Pound, "Promise or Bargain?," 33 *Tulane L. Rev.* 455 (1959).

8. "It is an elementary principle that the law will not enter into an inquiry as to the adequacy of the consideration." 1 Williston §115, at 454, citing Westlake v. Adams, 5 C.B. (n.s.) 248. See 1 Williston §115 and 1 Corbin §127 for numerous examples of consideration considered inadequate but held sufficient. See also *Restatement* (1st) §81 and (2d) §79. The commentators as well as the cases agree in deriving the law's decision not to engage in such "objective" valuation from the freedom of the parties to set their own values and draw their own contract. See also Professor Atiyah's account of the historical origins of the adequacy doctrine, which traces it directly to the complex of notions that underlie the freedom of contract. *The Rise and Fall of Freedom of Contract* 448-451 (Oxford, 1979).

9. 124 N.Y. 538, 27 N.E. 256 (1891).

10. Based on ill. 5, *Restatement* (2d) §71.

11. Id., at comment b. See also Fischer v. Union Trust Co., 138 Mich. 612, 101 N.W. 852 (1904); 1 Corbin §118; 1 Williston §111.

12. See John Dawson, *Gifts and Promises* 199-207 (New Haven, 1980) and particularly at 203 where Dawson disposes of Gilmore's "surprising . . . suggestion" that the bargain theory was invented by Holmes.

13. *The Common Law* 292-293 (Boston, 1881).

14. Case III is based on Wood v. Lucy, Lady Duff-Gordon, 222 N.Y. 88, 118 N.E. (1917) (Cardozo, J.), although Cardozo implied a promise by the agent to make reasonable efforts. The general problem of which the option-to-agent cases are an instance is generally known as the problem of mutuality of obligation. See *Restatement* (2d) §79 (c) and comment f.

15. See Arthur Corbin, "The Effect of Options on Consideration," 34 *Yale L. J.* 571 (1925); Corbin, "Nonbinding Promises as Consideration," 26 *Colum. L. Rev.* 550 (1926).

16. Case IV is based on Newman & Snell's State Bank v. Hunter, 243

Mich. 331, 220 N.W. 665 (1928). Williston regards this celebrated case as an anomalous violation of the doctrine of adequacy. Corbin straightforwardly attacks the result in his most magisterial phrase: "This is believed to be erroneous." 1 Corbin §127, note 83. The "market value" of the note is of no relevance, if the widow bargained for it, and the bank did not have to turn it over.

17. Case V is based on Zabella v. Pakel, 242 F.2d 452 (7th Cir. 1958). See *Restatement* (2d) §82, 83.

18. Mills v. Wyman, 3 Pick. 207 (Mass. 1825).

19. Webb v. McGowin, 27 Ala. App. 82, 168 So. 196 (1935).

20. Lingenfelder v. Wainwright Brewery Co., 103 Mo. 578, 15 S.W. 844 (1891).

21. Linz v. Schuck, 106 Md. 220, 67 A.A. 286 (1907).

22. Based on Foakes v. Beer, 9 A.C. 605 (House of Lords 1884).

23. The rule in Foakes v. Beer, while generally adhered to, has given rise to much criticism and opposition. See note 6 supra for statutory incursions upon it. Williston accepts this case wholeheartedly (1 Williston §120) and considers it merely a particularly clear instance of the pre-existing duty rule (see 1 Williston §120, §130A, at 542). It has been argued persuasively that this now-standard interpretation is in fact a misinterpretation of the leading cases. See James Barr Ames, "Two Theories of Consideration," 12 *Harv. L. R.* 515 (1899) and Merton Ferson, "The Rule in *Foakes v. Beer*," 31 Yale L. J. 15 (1926).

24. See Dawson, supra note 12, at 220-221; Ames, supra note 23, at 528; Lon Fuller, "Consideration and Form," *Colum. L. Rev.* 799, 818; and Joseph Beale, "Notes on Consideration," 17 *Harv. L. Rev.* 71, 71-72. Perhaps the clearest and most elegant exposition of this point, however, is Corbin's discussion at 1A Corbin §172.

25. See Samuel Williston, "Successive Promises of the Same Performance," 5 *Harv. L. Rev.* 27 (1894).

26. See Schwartzreich v. Baumanbasch, Inc., 231 N.Y. 196, 131 N.E. 887 (1921); 1 Williston §130A, at 540: "If for a single moment the parties were free from the original contract so that each of them could refuse to enter into any bargain whatever relating to the same subject matter, a subsequent agreement on any terms would be good."

27. Dawson, supra note 12.

28. Vol. VII (forthcoming), and see von Mehren, "Civil Law Analogues to Consideration," 72 *Harv. L. Rev.* 1009 (1959).

29. The sterility notion receives its classical statement in Claude Bufnoir, *Propriété et Contrat* 487 (Paris, 1900).

30. See generally Goetz and Scott, supra note 7, at 1265-1266; Eisenberg, supra note 7, at 4.

31. See Kant, *The Metaphysical Elements of Justice.* In economic terms both gifts and promises are Pareto-efficient transactions. See Harold Hochman and James Rogers, "Pareto Optimal Redistribution," 59 *Am. Econ. Rev.* 542 (1969).

32. 41 *Colum. L. Rev.* 799 (1941). See also Edwin Patterson, "An

Apology for Consideration," 58 *Colum. L. Rev.* 929 (1958); Atiyah, supra note 8.

33. For a less sanguine view, see Pound, supra note 7 at 455: "While the progress of the law had been more and more toward what had been taken to be the moral position that promises, as such, ought to be kept, and while until recently the law throughout the world had seemed to come almost (one might all but say substantially) to that position, there has begun a noticeable relaxation of the strict moral doctrine as to the obligation of intentional and advised promise. From antiquity the moral obligation to keep a promise had been a cardinal tenet of ethical philosophers, publicists, and philosophical jurists. . .

"Today, what we were taking to be the last step in bringing the law of contracts into complete accord with the precept of morals has been, at least for the time being, arrested and we are told that the supposed moral foundation is illusory. Men are not to be bound by promises. They are only to be held to bargains. The Marxian economic interpretation, the rise of the service state, and the humanitarian theory of liability, in different ways and in varying degrees, have seemed to be leading to a radically different view of the significance of a promise . . ."

## 4. ANSWERING A PROMISE: OFFER AND ACCEPTANCE

1. Karl Llewellyn, "On Our Case-Law of Contract: Offer and Acceptance, I, 48 *Yale L. J.* 1, 32 (1938). See also Llewellyn, "On Our Case-Law of Contract: Offer and Acceptance, II," 48 *Yale L. J.* 779 (1939).

2. For this point and the argument derived from it I am indebted to Robert Nozick.

3. That one cannot contract with oneself is universally agreed. See *Restatement* (1st) §15; 1 Williston §18, at 32; and 1 Corbin §55. Corbin, Williston, and *Restatement* (2d) §9 also agree in deriving this conclusion from the nature of promising. See 1 Corbin §55, at 233; 1 Williston §18, at 32; and 1 Williston §1; and *Restatement* (2d) §9, comment a.

That a legally enforceable promise must be made *to* someone is also universally agreed. See *Restatement* (1st) and (2d) §23: Only the person to whom the offer (promise) is made can accept it. For the rule that the offer must be communicated to the promisee see *Restatement* (1st) §23, 1 Williston §33, and 1 Corbin §59; but for some important exceptions see 1 Corbin §59 and 1 Williston §35. For the rule that offeree knowledge of the offer is required see *Restatement* (1st) §23 and (2d) §23, 1 Corbin §59, and 1 Williston §33B, and note exceptions.

4. Hugo Grotius, *Jure de Belli et Pacis*, bk. II, ch. XI, §§1-4 and 14-15 (Oxford, 1925); Samuel von Pufendorf, *Of the Law of Nature and Nations*, bk. III, ch. VI, §15; bk. III, ch. V, §§7 and 9-11 (London, 1729); *Restatement* (1st) §20; *Restatement* (2d) §18; 1 Williston §64. What is required is the promisee's *intentional* acceptance, intention being objectively understood. See *Restatement* (1st) §20, 1 Williston §66. See 1 Corbin §58 and 1 Corbin §62 for some exceptions to this rule, and 1 Corbin §58 for a good discussion of

promisee's *motive* in accepting (and compare 1 Corbin §84: "grumbling acceptance"). See 1 Corbin §67, 1 Williston §§68, 70 and *Restatement* (1st) §56 for the conditions governing and requirement of notice of acceptance to the offeror. See 1 Corbin §§72-73, 75, 1 Williston §§91-91D, and *Restatement* (1st) §§71-72 for discussions of the circumstances under which offeree silence will count as acceptance; offeree acceptance of a proffered benefit for which he knows payment is expected is the paradigm case.

For a discussion of the concept of acceptance in civil law, see Arthur von Mehren, *The Civil Law System* 465-474 (Boston, 1957). The seventeenth-century Scottish jurist Lord Stair (James Dalrymple) held that promises are binding without acceptance, though contracts in general are not. *The Institutions of Scotland*, bk. I, tit. 10, §§1-4 (Edinburgh, 1954).

5. See A. W. B. Simpson, *A History of the Common Law of Contract* 475-485 (Oxford, 1975) and Patrick Atiyah, *The Rise and Fall of Freedom of Contract* 413-414 (Oxford, 1979).

6. Lawrence v. Fox, 20 N.Y. 268 (1859), discussed at 4 Corbin §788. For summary statements of the basic rule on third-party enforcement see 2 Williston §§356, 361, 368; 4 Corbin §774; *Restatement* (1st) §§135, 136, and (2d) §304, 305.

7. See 2 Williston §§396-397 and 4 Corbin §§813-815 for discussions of the rules governing discharge or variation of the promise by the promisee, and of the reasons behind these. See also *Restatement* (1st) §§142-143 and (2d) §311. A leading case for the proposition that mere assent by the beneficiary cuts off the promisee's power to discharge is Copeland v. Beard, 217 Ala. 216, 115 So. 389 (1928). See also William Page, "The Power of Contracting Parties to Alter a Contract for Rendering Performance to a Third Person," 12 *Wis. L. Rev.* 141, 160 (1937).

8. See note 4 supra.

9. See *Restatement* (1st) §§20, 29, 1 Williston §§36, 36A; and 1 Corbin §§62-66, 72, 77.

10. For the notion of an offer as a conditional promise see *Restatement* (1st) and (2d) §24; 1 Williston 24A, 25 and 1 Corbin §11; Llewellyn, supra note 1; George Goble, "Is an Offer a Promise?," 22 *Ill. L. Rev.* 567 (1928); Samuel Williston, "Reply," 22 *Ill. L. Rev.* 788 (1928).

Atiyah argues that both the implied conditioning of the defendant's promise upon performance of the plaintiff's and the creation of the rules of offer and acceptance were aspects of the triumph of the executory agreement as the paradigm of contractual liability in the nineteenth century. Supra note 5, at 208-212, 424-428, 446-448.

11. See 1 Williston §73 and 1 Corbin §§82, 86.

12. *Restatement* (2d) §24, comment a, §35(1)(c), §41; 1 Williston §55; 1 Corbin §38; Grant Gilmore, *The Death of Contract* 28-30, 76-77 (Columbus, 1974) for discussion of the leading case for this proposition, Dickinson v. Dodds, 2 Ch. D. 463 (C.A. 1876).

13. See UCC §2-205 and chapter 3 supra, at notes 3 and 30.

14. See Wesley Hohfeld, "Fundamental Jural Relations Contrasted with One Another," 23 *Yale L. J.* 28, 49 (1913).

15. See *Restatement* (2d) §§38(2), 59; 1 Corbin §§82-94.

16. Adams v. Lindsell, 1 B. & Ald. 681, 106 Eng. Rep. 250 (K.B. 1818); *Restatement* (2d) §63.

17. A *Summary of the Law of Contracts* 20-21 (2d ed. Boston 1880).

18. See to this effect, 1 Corbin §78 at 336-338; Llewellyn, supra note 1, at 795. Langdell, supra note 17, thought such arguments "irrelevant."

19. See *Restatement* (2d) §§40, 63; Lon Fuller and Melvin Eisenberg, *Basic Contract Law* 349-351 (3rd ed. St. Paul 1972).

20. See Tinn v. Hoffman, 29 L.T.R. (n.s.) 271 (Exch. 1873); 1 Corbin §59 at 247-248; Arthur Corbin, "Offer and Acceptance and Some of the Resulting Legal Relations," 26 *Yale L. J.* 169, 182-183 (1917).

21. I. Maurice Wormser, "The True Conception of Unilateral Contracts," 26 *Yale L. J.* 136 (1916), recanted at 3 *J. Legal Educ.* 146 (1950).

22. *Restatement* (2d) §45 protects B by creating an option contract, which binds A to keep his offer open until B completes performance.

23. See footnote p.45 supra.

24. The leading case protecting General Contractor's reliance in such a situation under the principle of *Restatement* (1st) §90 is Drennan v. Star Paving Co., 51 Cal. 2d 409, 333 P.2d 757 (1958). *Restatement* (2d) §87(2) creates an option contract in General's favor "to the extent necessary to avoid injustice."

## 5. GAPS

1. Grant Gilmore, *The Death of Contract* 87 et seq. (Columbus, 1974); Duncan Kennedy, "Form and Substance in Private Law Adjudication," 89 *Harv. L. Rev.* 1685, 1719-1720, 1725-1737 (1976); Karl Klare, review of C. L. Knapp, *Problems in Contract Law: Cases and Materials*, 54 *N.Y.U. L. Rev.* 876, 887 (1979).

2. See *Restatement* (1st) §502, "When Mistake Makes a Contract Voidable." See also *Restatement* (1st) §454, "Definition of Impossibility"; UCC §2-615; *Restatement* (2d) §§151-3, "Mistake"; *Restatement* (2d) §261, "Discharge by Supervening Impracticability"; *Restatement* (2d) ch. II, "Impracticability of Performance and Frustration of Purpose" (tentative draft no. 9, 1974); John Dawson, "Effects of Inflation on Private Contracts: Germany, 1914-1924," 33 *Mich. L. Rev.* 171 (1934); John Dawson and Frank Cooper, "The Effect of Inflation on Private Contracts: U.S. — The Inflation in the North, 1861-1879," 33 *Mich. L. Rev.* 706 (1935); Edwin Patterson, "The Apportionment of Business Risks through Legal Devices," 24 *Colum. L. Rev.* 335 (1924); Richard Posner and Andrew Rosenfield, "Impossibility and Related Doctrines in Contract Law: An Economic Analysis," 6 *J. Leg. Stud.* 83 (1977).

3. 19 T.L.R. 434 (K.B. 1903).

4. 2 K.B. 740 (C.A. 1903). The coronation was scheduled for 26 June 1902. The king's illness was announced on 24 June and he was operated on the same day. The coronation took place on 9 August.

5. 3 Best and S. 826 (Q.B. 1863).

6. Gilmore, supra note 1, at 81, and note 216 referring to Bell v. Lever Brothers, Inc., L.R. 1932 A.C. 161 (1931) (Atkin, J.).

7. 64 Wis. 265, 25 N.W. 42 (1885).

8. 66 Mich. 568, 33 N.W. 919 (1887).

9. 2 Hurl. and C. 906 (Exch. 1864).

10. See George Gardner, "An Inquiry into the Principles of the Law of Contracts," 46 *Harv. L. Rev.* 1, 33 (1932) ("limited responsibility for apparent promise"); Oliver Wendell Holmes, "The Theory of Legal Interpretation" 12 *Harv. L. Rev.* 417, 419 (1899); Clarke Whittier, "The Restatement of Contracts and Mutual Assent," 17 *Calif. L. Rev.* 441 (1929), whose conclusion is essentially the same as my proposal in this chapter; William Young, "Equivocation in the Making of Agreements" 64 *Colum. L. Rev.* 619 (1964); Dadourian Export Corp. v. United States, 291 F.2d 178, 187 n.4 (2d Cir. 1961) (Friendly, J., dissenting).

11. Blackburn, J., in Taylor v. Caldwell, supra note 5; William Anson, *Law of Contract* 506-507 (25th ed. Oxford, 1979); 3 Corbin §565; 6 Corbin §1331 (1946).

12. The fons et origo is Ludwig Wittgenstein, *Philosophical Investigations* §§138-326 (Anscombe transl. Oxford, 1953). The subsequent literature is enormous. For a recent commentary, see Crispin Wright, *Wittgenstein on the Foundations of Mathematics* ch. 2 (Cambridge, 1980). See also H. L. A. Hart, "Positivism and the Separation of Law and Morals," 71 *Harv. L. Rev.* 593 (1958); Ronald Dworkin, "How to Read the Civil Rights Act," *The New York Review of Books*, Dec. 20, 1979, at 37.

13. This concept of interpretation is analogous to what Ronald Dworkin argues is the process of judicial interpretation and elaboration of statutes and precedents. *Taking Rights Seriously* ch. 4, app., 338-345 (rev. ed. Cambridge, 1978). This conception of interpretation was adumbrated by Lon Fuller, in *The Law in Quest of Itself* (Evanston, 1940) and in "Reason and Fiat in Case Law," 59 *Harv. L. Rev.* 376 (1946).

14. 1 Williston §94 at 339: "It follows that the test of the true interpretation of an offer or acceptance is not what the party making it thought he meant, but what a reasonable person in the position of the parties would have thought it meant"; see also Gilmore, supra note 1, at 41-43; Oliver Wendall Holmes, *The Common Law* 230 (Boston, 1881).

15. *Restatement* (1st) §§70-71, §503; *Restatement* (2d) §153; Edwin Patterson, "Equitable Relief for Unilateral Mistakes," 28 *Colum. L. Rev.* 859 (1928).

16. This case is based on Smith v. Zimbalist, 2 Cal. App.2d 324, 38 P.2d 170 (1934), hearing denied Jan. 17, 1935, in which relief was granted, but only because the court found that the seller's receipt giving the makers' names constituted a warranty (i.e. contractual guarantee) of authenticity. Compare *Restatement* (1st) §503, ill. 2.

17. See Patterson, supra note 15; Whittier, supra note 10.

18. See M. F. Kemper Construction Co. v. City of Los Angeles, 37 Cal.2d 696, 235 P.2d 7 (1951).

19. See Elsinore Union Elementary School District v. Kastorff, 54 Cal.2d 380, 353 P.2d 713 (1960).

20. 20 Minn. 494 (1874). See also Paradine v. Jane, 82 Eng. Rep. 519 (K.B. 1647); Gilmore, supra note 1, at 44-46.

21. See 18 Williston §§1963-1964.

22. See Patrick Atiyah, *The Rise and Fall of Freedom of Contract* 436-438 (Oxford, 1979); Whittier, supra note 10.

23. Gilmore, supra note 1, at 140. See also Morton Horwitz, *The Transformation of American Law* 181-185 (Cambridge, 1977).

24. See Herbert Spencer, *Principles of Ethics,* pt. IV, *Justice* ch. 3 (London, 1891). There are echoes of this view in Friedrich Hayek, *The Constitution of Liberty* ch. 3 (Chicago, 1960).

25. See Julius Stone, *Legal System and Lawyer's Reasoning* 185-192, 212-218 (Stanford, 1964); Max Weber, *On Law in Economy and Society* 62, 277, 354 (Rheinstein ed., Cambridge, 1954).

26. "No Right Answer?," 53 *N.Y.U. L. Rev.* 1, 16-23 (1978).

27. Dworkin gives the most closely argued and philosophically sophisticated version of a conception of law that was at least adumbrated by Lon Fuller, supra note 13, and by Henry Hart and Albert Sacks, *The Legal Process* pt. I, ch. 3 (Cambridge, 1958). Because this view of law is necessary to save liberal theory from the absurdities of positivism, critics of liberalism such as Roberto Unger, *Knowledge and Politics* 94-97 (New York, 1975) and Kennedy, supra note 1, at 1764-1766 are particularly vehement in their denunciation of it. See also note 22 to chapter 6 infra.

28. Cf. Angus v. Scully, 176 Mass. 357, 57 N.E. 674 (1900); Carroll v. Bowersock, 100 Kan. 270, 164 P. 143 (1917).

29. Cf. Fibrosa Spolka Akcyjna v. Fairbairn Lawson Combe Barbour, Ltd., [1943] A.C. 32.

30. Marks Realty Co. v. Hotel Hermitage Co., 170 App. Div. 484, 156 N.Y.S. 179 (1915).

31. I am grateful to Duncan Kennedy for pointing out the importance of this concept. Supra note 1, at 1717-1718.

32. R. A. Brown, *The Law of Personal Property* (3d ed. Chicago, 1975) §3.2. The American law is that the money would go to whichever of the two spending the night found it and took it into possession with intent to keep it. The finder could, of course, share it with his companion if he desired. According to the English rule it would probably go to the owner of the inn, though it might go to the man or the woman if the court decided the owner had waived control of the drawer involved to them.

33. See Grant Gilmore and Charles Black, *The Law of Admiralty* (2d ed. Mineola, N.Y., 1975) ch. V, "General Average." The admiralty rule is that the loss should be totaled and distributed among shippers and shipowner.

34. This allegorical figure is central to Bruce Ackerman's *Social Justice in the Liberal State* (New Haven, 1980).

35. *Restatement* (2d) §272(2): "In any case governed by the rules stated in this chapter [chapter 11, "Impracticability of Performance and Frustration of Purpose"], if those rules together with the rules stated in prospective chapter 16 will not avoid injustice, the court may . . . supply a term which is reasonable in the circumstances."

36. See Charles Fried, *Right and Wrong* chs. 5, 6 (Cambridge, 1978) for a statement of position and a review of the literature on this point.

37. See id. chs. 2, 5, 7.

38. This idea of a common enterprise as a basis for sharing may also be behind the law's increasing willingness to allow contribution among joint tortfeasors and, by extension, behind the reduction of damages in a tort action where both plantiff and defendant are found to have been at fault.

## 6. GOOD FAITH

1. See John Dawson, "Economic Duress: An Essay in Perspective," 45 *Mich. L. Rev.* 253 (1947); Lawrence M. Friedman, *Contract Law in America* 98-105, 190-194 (Madison, 1965); Grant Gilmore, *The Death of Contract* 94-96 (Columbus, 1974); Robert Lee Hale, *Freedom through Law: Public Control of Private Governing Power* pt. I, ch. 1, 3-12 and pt. II, ch. 7, 109-136 (New York, 1952); Hale, "Bargaining, Duress and Economic Liberty," 43 *Colum. L. Rev.* 603 (1943); Hale, "Coercion and Distribution in a Supposedly Noncoercive State," 38 *Pol. Sci. Q.* 470 (1923); Duncan Kennedy, "Form and Substance in Private Law Adjudication," 89 *Harv. L. Rev.* 1685, 1725-1726, 1735-1737, 1778 (1976).

2. See, e.g., Anthony Kronman, "Contract Law and Distributive Justice," 89 *Yale L. J.* 472, 486 (1980).

3. For the statement of Maine's thesis see Henry Maine, *Ancient Law* 170 (London, 1861). For the retreat, see Ian Macneil, *Contracts, Exchange Transactions and Relationships* 346-502 (2d ed. Mineola, N.Y., 1978); Macneil, "The Many Futures of Contract," 47 *S. Cal. L. Rev.* 691, 693-696 and passim (1974); Macneil, "Whither Contracts?," 21 *J. Legal Educ.* 403, 404-406 (1969); Lon Fuller, *The Morality of Law* 27-30, 42-43 (New Haven, 1963); Fuller and William Perdue, "The Reliance Interest in Contract Damages (pt. 1)," 46 *Yale L. J.* 52, 70-71 (1936); Gilmore, supra note 1, at 94-96; Friedrich Kessler and Grant Gilmore, *Contracts* pt. I, ch. 11 (2d ed. Boston, 1970); Kessler and Edith Fine, "*Culpa in Contrahendo*, Bargaining in Good Faith, and Freedom of Contract: A Comparative Study," 77 *Harv. L. Rev.* 401, 404-405, 407-412, 448-449 (1964); Roscoe Pound, "The Law as Developed in Juristic Thought," 30 *Harv. L. Rev.* 201, 210 (1917). See also Patrick Atiyah, *The Rise and Fall of Freedom of Contract* 716-737 (Oxford, 1979); Emile Durkheim, *The Division of Labor in Society* ch. 7 (Simpson trans. New York, 1933).

4. See Kennedy, supra note 1, at 1713-1716, 1717-1722, 1728-1729, 1733-1737.

5. For discussions of formalism, see Kennedy, supra note 1, at 1729-1730, 1737, 1770; Kennedy, "Legal Formality," 2 *J. Leg. Stud.* 351, 359-360 (1973); Atiyah, supra note 3, at 338-448; Herbert Hart, "Positivism and the Separation of Law and Morals," 71 *Harv. L. Rev.* 593, 608-613 (1958); Morton Horwitz, *The Transformation of American Law* 201, 253-266 (Cambridge, 1977); Horwitz, "The Rise of Legal Formalism," 19 *Am. J. Leg. Hist.* 251 (1975); A. W. B. Simpson, "The Horwitz Thesis and the History of

Contracts," 46 *U. Chi. L. Rev.* 533, 534 (1979) (formalism described as "that most ill-defined of legal ailments").

6. See A. C. Pigou, *The Economics of Welfare* 82-97 (4th ed. London, 1962); John Rawls, *A Theory of Justice* ch. 5. (Cambridge, 1971).

7. See UCC §1-201 (19) (" 'Good faith' means honesty in fact in the conduct or transaction concerned"); UCC §2-103 (b) (" 'Good faith' in the case of a merchant means honesty in fact and the observance of reasonable commercial standards of fair dealing in the trade"); E. Allan Farnsworth, "Good Faith Performance and Commercial Reasonableness under the Uniform Commercial Code," 30 *U. Chi. L. Rev.* 666 (1963); Russell A. Eisenberg, "Good Faith under the Code," 54 *Marquette L. Rev.* 1 (1971); Robert S. Summers, "Good Faith in General Contact Law and the Sales Provisions of the Uniform Commercial Code," 54 *Va. L. Rev.* 195 (1968); Kessler and Fine, supra note 3. See also J. F. Burrows, "Contractual Cooperation and Implied Terms," 31 *Mod. L. Rev.* 390 (1968) for an interesting discussion of a somewhat broader notion of good faith, an implied duty of cooperation.

8. Atiyah, supra note 3, at 345-358.

9. 56 Wash.2d 449, 353 P.2d 672 (1960). See the discussion of this case in Anthony Kronman, "Mistake, Disclosure, Information and the Law of Contracts," 7 *J. Legal Stud.* 1, 24-25 (1978).

10. See *Restatement* (1st) §§470, 476; (2d) §§159, 162-164; William Prosser, *Law of Torts* §§105, 106 (4th ed. St. Paul, 1971).

11. Fried, *Right and Wrong* ch. 3 (Cambridge, 1978).

12. See Kronman, supra note 2, at 481-483, 490.

13. Cf. the use of a similar example in Kronman, supra note 9, at 18-27.

14. See Fried, supra note 11, at chs. 2, 3, 7.

15. Prosser, supra note 10, at 695-699: "The law appears to be working toward the ultimate conclusion that full disclosure of all material facts must be made whenever elementary fair conduct demands it." See 12 Williston §1498 at 386 for an argument that the farmer should be given relief. See also Leo Bearman, "Caveat Emptor in Sales of Realty: Recent Assault upon the Rule," 14 *Vand. L. Rev.* 541 (1961); W. Page Keeton, "Fraud, Concealment and Non-Disclosure," 15 *Tex. L. Rev.* 1 (1936); Keeton, "Rights of Disappointed Purchasers," 32 *Tex. L. Rev.* 1 (1953). But see note 17 infra and accompanying text.

16. Cf. chapter 5 supra, at notes 18, 19, and accompanying text.

17. See Leitch Gold Mines, Ltd. v. Texas Gulf Sulphur, 1 Ont. Rep. 469, 492-493 (1969): TGS was only doing "what any prudent mining company would have done to acquire property in which it knew a very promising anomaly lay" when it purchased property "without causing the prospective vendors to suspect that a discovery had been made." TGS got, for $18,000, mining rights worth $100,000,000. See also Laidlaw v. Orgon, 2 Wheat. (4 U.S.) 178 (1817) (Marshall, C. J.). For a discussion of these cases see Kronman supra note 9, at 20-21, and Morton Shulman, *The Billion Dollar Windfall* (New York, 1969).

18. See Kronman, supra note 2, at 478-480, 486.

19. See *Restatement* (1st) §472(c) and comment c; *Restatement* (2d) §303

(tent. draft no. 12, March 1977); 12 Williston §1499 at 390-393; *Restatement* (2d) Torts §551; Prosser, supra note 10, §106 at 697.

20. See Kennedy, supra note 1, at 1750-1751, 1760-1762, 1772-1774.

21. See Ronald Dworkin, *Taking Rights Seriously* 297-311 (Cambridge, 1978).

22. That contract as promise, that is, the liberal theory of contract and the liberal theory of law in general, are precluded from elaborating obligation in this way, that they are relegated to some kind of formalistic, mechanical mode of elaboration only, is a canard given currency among legal scholars by Roberto Unger, *Knowledge and Politics* ch. 2 (New York, 1975). This commitment to formalism is said to depend in turn on a commitment to something called the subjectivity of values. Neither this concept of subjectivity of values nor the objectivity contrasted to it is given a clear sense, but whatever vague sense it has is plainly inapplicable to classical liberals like Locke or Kant or modern liberals like Rawls, Nozick, or Dworkin, all of whom argue for theories in which rights figure as objective entities. Unger makes his claim about liberalism only by the astonishing procedure of denying that it depends for its truth on what particular liberals have actually written. *Knowledge and Politics* 7-12. For a fuller discussion of this method, see Charles Fried, "The Laws of Change," 9 *J. Legal Stud.* 335, 350-351 (1980); and Anthony Kronman, review of Unger's *Knowledge and Politics*, 61 *Minn. L. Rev.* 167, 191-194 (1976). In fact Unger's account is an imaginative and powerful reconstruction primarily of Hobbesian thought, but hardly of liberalism in general. Recently a number of legal writers have attacked liberalism by attributing to it doctrines like formalism and subjectivity of values, sometimes giving as authority Unger's account. Examples are Gerald E. Frug, "The City as a Legal Concept," 93 *Harv. L. Rev.* 1057, 1074 (1980); Kennedy, supra note 1, at 1732, 1766-1771; Kennedy, supra note 5, at 353 n.7, 361-365; Karl Klare, "Judicial Deradicalization of the Wagner Act and the Origins of Modern Legal Consciousness, 1937-41," 62 *Minn. L. Rev.* 265, 276-277 (1978); Klare, "Review, Contracts Jurisprudence and the First Year Casebook," 54 *N.Y.U. L. Rev.* 876, 881, 889 n.69 (1980) (citing Kennedy, who cites Unger); William H. Simon, "Homo Psychologius: Notes on a New Legal Formalism," 32 *Stan. L. Rev.* 487, 493 (1980). For just one recent example of an eminently liberal contemporary political theorist who rejects and argues against both Hobbes and Hobbesian (*but not liberal*) postulates of the subjectivity of values and of the vanity of general moral terms such as justice and cruelty, see Michael Walzer, *Just and Unjust Wars* ch. 1 (New York, 1977).

23. The most arresting statement of this conception of the legal process is Ronald Dworkin's, supra note 21, ch. 4, "Hard Cases." As suggested earlier, this harks back particularly to the more intuitive work of Lon Fuller.

24. See J. F. Burrows, supra note 7, esp. 395-405 for a discussion of the extent to which each party has a "duty to cooperate" in the contractual undertaking. See generally Kessler and Gilmore, supra note 3, at 944-976; "Good Faith Performance"; Kessler and Fine, supra note 3.

25. See Kennedy, supra note 1, at 1721.

26. Unpublished manuscript, part of work in progress on legal doctrine.
27. 204 N.Y. 96, 97 N.E. 472 (1912).
28. 272 Pa. 172, 116 A. 150 (1922).
29. 341 Mass. 684, 171 N.E.2d 865 (1961).
30. See Arthur Corbin, "The Effect of Options on Consideration," 34 *Yale L. J.* 571, 579-583 (1925); Kessler and Gilmore, supra note 3, at 337-361, "Requirements Contracts and Mutuality"; Karl Llewellyn, *Cases and Materials on the Law of Sales* 452 (Chicago, 1930); Edwin Patterson, "Illusory Promises and Promisor Options," 6 *Iowa L. Bull.* 129, 209 (1921).
31. UCC §2-306, comment 2: "A shutdown by a requirements buyer for lack of orders might be permissible when a shutdown merely to curtail losses would not. The essential test is whether a party is acting in good faith . . ." See also 3 Corbin §569 and 1 Williston §104A; City of Lakeland, Fla. v. Union Oil Co. of Cal., 352 F. Supp. 758 (D. Fla. 1973) (increase in amount of energy sold by city to surrounding communities was too great to stay within good faith limits on contract with oil company to furnish all oil used by city for electric generating facility); "Note, Requirements Contracts under Uniform Commercial Code," 102 *U. Pa. L. Rev.* 654 (1954).
32. Ludwig Wittgenstein, *Philosophical Investigations* (Anscombe trans. 3d. ed., Oxford, 1958), p.33e, quoted in Lon Fuller and Melvin Eisenberg, *Basic Contract Law* 808-809 (3rd ed. St. Paul, 1972). See also Herbert Hart, "Positivism and the Separation of Law and Morals," 71 *Harv. L. Rev.* 593, 608-612 (1958).

## 7. DURESS AND UNCONSCIONABILITY

1. UCC §2-302, Unconscionable Contract or Clause, comment 1: "The principle is one of the prevention of oppression and unfair surprise and not of disturbance of allocation of risks because of superior bargaining power." See Arthur Leff, "Unconscionability and the Code: The Emperor's New Clause," 115 *U. Pa. L. Rev.* 485 (1967), introducing the important distinction between procedural and substantive unconscionability, and suggesting that the whole notion is incoherent. Contra, P. Ellinghaus, "In Defense of Unconscionability," 78 *Yale L. J.* 757 (1969). See also Norman Jaffee, "Definition and Interpretation of Unconscionable Contracts under the Code," 58 *Dick. L. Rev.* 161 (1954); John Murray, "Unconscionability: Unconscionability," 31 *U. Pitt. L. Rev.* 1 (1969).
2. See *Restatement* (1st) §20, comment a (intent to assent to the agreement, and presence of a conscious will to do the acts manifesting assent); 1 Corbin §11 at 25.
3. See Anthony Kronman, "Contract Law and Distributive Justice," 89 *Yale L. J.* 472, 477-478 (1980). See also John Dalzell, "Duress by Economic Pressure," 20 *N.Car. L. Rev.* 237, 239-240 (1942); John Dawson, "Economic Duress: An Essay in Perspective," 45 *Mich. L. Rev.* 253, 267 (1947); Robert Lee Hale, "Bargaining, Duress and Economic Liberty," 43 *Colum. L. Rev.* 603, 616-617 (1943).
4. Compare David Hume, *An Enquiry Concerning the Human Under-*

*standing* 80-103 (Oxford, 1902); W. D. Ross, *Foundations of Ethics*, "Indeterminacy and Indeterminism," 222-251 (Oxford, 1939).

5. See materials cited in note 3 supra and note 1 to chapter 6 supra. See also Karl Marx, *Capital* 81-96 (Moore and Aveling trans. New York, 1906); Roscoe Pound, "Liberty of Contract," 18 *Yale L. J.* 454, 482-483 (1909); Max Weber, 2 *Economy and Society* 729-731 (Roth, Wittich eds. New York, 1968).

6. See *Restatement* (1st) §492; *Restatement* (2d) §§174-176; *Restatement of Restitution* §70. See also 13 Williston §§1603, 1605; Tallmadge v. Robinson, 158 Ohio St. 333, 109 N.E.2d 496 (1952) (threat of half-sister to allege illicit relations with her father to bring odium on the family); Stevenson v. Sherman 231 S.W.2d 506 (Tex. Civ. App. 1950) (threat to remove candidate from ballot if he did not pay over 25 percent of his campaign funds). See generally Arthur Leff, "Injury, Ignorance, and Spite: The Dynamics of Coercive Collection," 80 *Yale L. J.* 1 (1970).

7. See 13 Williston §§1601-1602 for a discussion of the gradual enlargement of the legal concept of duress; Dawson, supra note 3, at 255; *Restatement* (2d) Torts §892B (3), and comment j; American Law Institute, Model Penal Code §2.09 (proposed official draft, May 1962) (this section adopts the standard of a "person of reasonable firmness"). See also Rollin M. Perkins, *Criminal Law* 951-955 (2d ed. Mineola, N.Y., 1969); Ian H. Dennis, "Duress, Murder and Criminal Responsibility," 96 *L. Q. Rev.* 208 (1980).

8. Robert Nozick, "Coercion," *Philosophy, Science and Method: Essays in Honor of Ernest Nagel* 440-472 (Morgenbesser, Suppes, White eds. New York, 1969).

9. Based on Borough of Bradford v. Pickles, 3 Ch. 54 (1894), 1 Ch. 145 (1895), aff'd [1895] A. C. 587. See 5 Richard Powell and Patrick Rohan, *The Law of Real Property* §§711 and 725 (1980 ed.). (The legal disposition of this English case depends on whether the water in question is classified as a stream or as percolating waters; the latter but not the former can be appropriated altogether.)

10. See Dalzell, supra note 3, at 240 for a similar account; *Restatement* (2d) §176 focuses on wrongfulness of proposed acts. See also Dale v. Simon 267 S.W. 467, 470 (Tex.Com.App. 1924): "There can be no duress unless there is a threat to do some act which the party threatening has no legal right to do." (Williston reports that this leading case is often cited and constitutes the basic principle of duress. 13 Williston §1603, n. 9). See also Dawson, supra note 3, at 287-288, for a critical discussion of this formulation of duress.

11. See Richard Posner, *Economic Analysis of Law* 27-31 (2d. ed. Boston, 1977).

12. Charles Fried, *Right and Wrong* chs. 2 and 4 (Cambridge, 1978).

13. Powell and Rohan, supra note 9, at §726; VI-A *American Law of Property* §§28.66, 28.68 (Boston, 1954).

14. Morton Horwitz, *The Transformation of American Law* 34-42 (Cambridge, 1977).

15. See Bruce A. Ackerman, ed., *Economic Foundations of Property Law*

(Boston, 1975) for a useful collection of articles and references on these and related topics; Ackerman, *Private Property and the Constitution* (New Haven, 1977); Lawrence Carlyle Becker, *Property Rights: Philosophic Foundations* (London, 1977); Ronald H. Coase, "The Problem of Social Cost," 3 *J. L. and Econ.* 1 (1960); Harold Demsetz, "Toward a Theory of Property Rights," 57 *Am. Econ. Rev.* 347 (1967) (vol. 2, *Papers and Proceedings*); Frank I. Michelman, "Property, Utility, and Fairness: Comments on the Ethical Foundations of 'Just Compensation' Law," 80 *Harv. L. Rev.* 1165 (1968).

16. See Anthony Kronman, "Contract Law and Distributive Justice," 89 *Yale L. J.* 472, 495-7; Emile Durkheim, *The Division of Labor in Society* ch. 7 (Simpson trans. New York, 1933). Cf. Duncan Kennedy, "Form and Substance in Private Law Adjudication," 89 *Harv. L. Rev.* 1685, 1731-1732 (1976).

17. Compare Herman Melville, *Moby Dick* ch. 89, "Fast-fish and Loose-fish."

18. See Ronald Dworkin, *Taking Rights Seriously* chs. 4, 7, app. 297-311 (Cambridge, 1978); Fried, supra note 12, at ch. 4.

19. Adam Smith, 1 *An Inquiry into the Nature and Causes of the Wealth of Nations* 25-30, "Of the Principle which gives occasion to the Division of Labour" (Glasgow ed. Oxford, 1976) (how exchange, without any planning, gives rise to the great improvement in productive power previously described). Friedrich Hayek, *The Constitution of Liberty* chs. 2 and 3 (Chicago, 1960).

20. See Immanuel Kant, *The Metaphysical Elements of Justice* 35-37, 51-67 (Ladd trans. Indianapolis, 1965).

Thus I agree with Duncan Kennedy and Frank Michelman, "Are Property and Contract Efficient?," *Hofstra L. Rev.* (forthcoming), that the answer to their question is: not necessarily. Property and contract may or may not be efficient; they are right.

21. See Dworkin, supra note 18, at 297-311. Cf. Hayek, supra note 19, at ch. 14.

22. See Michelman, supra note 15, at 1229-1234, for an account of the importance of legal definitions of property interests, and of changes in such definitions.

23. Michael Graetz considers this argument in respect to changes in the tax law and reviews the literature in "Legal Transitions: The Case of Retroactivity in Income Tax Revision," 126 *U. Pa. L. Rev.* 47, 74-76 and n. 80 (1977).

24. This case is based on Jones v. Star Credit Corp., 59 Misc.2d 189, 298 N.Y.S.2d 264 (Sup. Ct., 1969). See also Williams v. Walker-Thomas Furniture Co., 121 U.S. App.D.C. 315, 350 F.2d 445 (D.C. Cir. 1965).

25. See N.Y. Workmen's Compensation Law §10 (McKinney) (employer liability for employee disability without regard to fault, except intoxication or willful injury); N.Y. Workmen's Compensation Law §11 (McKinney) (previously described liability of employer is exclusive and in place of common law right of action).

26. This case is based on Henningsen v. Bloomfield Motors, Inc., 32 N.J 358, 161 A.2d 69 (1960).

27. These and similar cases are discussed in Leff, supra note 1, passim.

28. See Richard A. Epstein, "Unconscionability: A Critical Reappraisal," 18 *J. L. and Econ.* 293, 305-315 (1975) for an interesting discussion of the economic and social backgrounds justifying contract terms now widely felt to be substantively unconscionable. See generally Lon Fuller and Melvin Eisenberg, *Basic Contract Law* 592-609 (3rd ed. St. Paul, 1972).

29. See Ronald Dworkin, "Liberalism," in *Public and Private Morality* (S. Hampshire ed., Cambridge, England, 1978); Fried, supra note 12, at ch. 5; Hayek, supra note 19, at 257; Richard A. Musgrave and Peggy B. Musgrave, *Public Finance in Theory and Practice* 12 (2d. ed. New York, 1976); John Rawls, *A Theory of Justice* ch. 5 (Cambridge, 1971); Thomas Scanlon, "Liberty, Contract and Contribution," in *Markets and Morals* (Dworkin, Bermant, Brown eds. Washington, 1977).

30. See Philip Areeda and Donald Turner, 2 *Antitrust Law* §§402b2, 402b3, 403c (Boston, 1978). Cf. Charles Goetz and Robert Scott, "Liquidated Damages, Penalties and the Just Compensation Principle: Some Notes on an Enforcement Model and a Theory of Efficient Breach," 77 *Colum. L. Rev.* 554, 558 (1977).

31. See e.g. 11 U.S.C. §522 (1978); Mass. Gen. Laws, Ann. ch. 235, §34 for enumeration of the exemptions. See Lawrence King, ed., 3 *Collier on Bankruptcy* §552-§522.31 (esp. §522.01, statutory history, and §522.02, exemptions generally).

32. 19 How. (60 U.S.) 150 (1856). See Grant Gilmore and Charles Black, *The Law of Admiralty* ch. 8 (2d ed. Mineola, N.Y., 1975) (esp. §8-1, The Nature of Salvage: What Property May Be Salved, and §8-8, The Salvage Award: How Computed, How Distributed). See also 13 Williston §1608 (Is Persuasion or Pressure of Circumstances Duress?).

33. 226 S.W.2d 673 (Tex.Civ.App. 1949).

34. Fried, supra note 12, at ch. 5; cf. Hayek, supra note 19, at 257.

35. Kant, *Groundwork of the Metaphysics of Morals* 90-91 (Paton trans., Harper Torchbooks ed. New York, 1964).

36. Fried, supra note 12, at ch. 7.

37. See Eric Mack, "Bad Samaritanism and the Causation of Harm," 9 *Phil. and Pub. Affairs* 230 (1980) (a good review of the literature, and criticism of the argument that the Bad Samaritan's omission is the *cause* of harm); Francis Bolen, "The Moral Duty to Aid Others as the Basis of Tort Liability," 47 *U. Pa. L. Rev.* 217 (1908) (rejecting the causal thesis above but arguing for a duty to rescue); A. M. Honoré, "Law, Morals, and Rescue," in *The Good Samaritan and the Law* (Ratcliffe ed. New York, 1966) (arguing for a duty to rescue); William Landes and Richard Posner, "Salvors, Finders, Good Samaritans, and Other Rescuers: An Economic Study of Law and Altruism," 7 *J. Legal Stud.* 83 (1978).

## 8. THE IMPORTANCE OF BEING RIGHT

1. There is a widespread view that it is irrational to allow large consequences to depend on small variations in the controlling circumstances. To

put this intuition more formally, it is irrational for the value of a function to vary discontinuously while its arguments vary continuously. This intuition is regularly invoked against deontological moral principles, which, for instance, forbid producing a good result by some described means but not by others—for examples, saving many lives by killing a few innocents—or which (like Rawls's second principle of justice) permit inequalities only so far as they improve the situation of the worst-off representative man, so that no amount of gain to the more fortunate justifies depressing the situation of the least. Underlying this intuition must be the implicit assumption that the ultimate measure of value is expressible as a single continuous quantity, of which Bentham's pleasure principle is the most familiar example; but the intuition is much more widespread than is explicit adherence to any such ultimate moral teleology. See Lon Fuller and William Perdue, "The Reliance Interest in Contract Damages: 2," 46 *Yale L. J.* 373, 419-420 (1937) for an example of the intuition. The intuition is implicit in much decision theory; see Howard Raiffa, *Decision Analysis* ch. 4 (Reading, Ma., 1968); and see the discussion and references in Amartya Sen, *Collective Choice and Social Welfare* ch. 3 (San Francisco, 1970). The most powerful statement against this intuitive view of rationality as continuous occurs in John Rawls, *A Theory of Justice* §§83, 84 (Cambridge, 1971). See also Robert Nozick, "Moral Complications and Moral Structures," 12 *Natural L. F.* 3 (1968).

2. See Bush v. Canfield, 2 Conn. 485 (1818). Plaintiff recovered full $5000 advance payment, even though, had the contract been fully performed, he would have suffered a loss of $3000 on the deal.

For an explication of the general principles of restitutionary recovery, see generally George Palmer, *The Law of Restitution* (Boston, 1978); Robert Goff and Gareth Jones, *The Law of Restitution* (2d ed. London, 1978); Robert Childress and Jack Garamella, "The Law of Restitution and the Reliance Interest in Contract," 64 *Nw. U. L. Rev.* 433 (1969); John Dawson, "Restitution or Damages?," 20 *Ohio St. L. J.* 145 (1959); E. Allan Farnsworth, "Legal Remedies for Breach of Contract," 70 *Colum. L. Rev.* 1145, 1148, 1175-1177 (1970); George Gardner, "An Inquiry into the Principles of the Law of Contracts," 46 *Harv. L. Rev.* 1, 15-18 (1932); Robert Nordstrom, "Restitution on Default and Article Two of the Uniform Commercial Code," 19 *Vand. L. Rev.* 1143 (1966).

3. See, e.g., Boomer v. Muir, 24 P.2d 570 (Cal.App. 1933), hearing dismissed; 5 Corbin §1112 (1964); John Calamari and Joseph Perillo, *The Law of Contracts* 547-575 (2d ed. St. Paul, 1977). Cf. Jerome Walsh, "Restitution-Availability as an Alternative Remedy Where Plaintiff Has Fully Performed a Contract to Provide Goods or Services," 57 *Mich. L. Rev.* 268 (1958).

4. See generally Goff and Jones, supra note 2, esp. ch. 23.

5. See Childress and Garamella, supra note 2, at 441; Joseph Perillo, "Restitution in a Contractual Context," 73 *Colum. L. Rev.* 1208, 1224-1225 (1973).

6. See the discussions of option contracts in chapter 3 supra, at 36, and chapter 4 supra, at 48.

7. Oliver Wendell Holmes, *The Common Law* 236 (1881, M. Howe ed. 1963). The increasing availability of specific performance and the doctrine of anticipatory breach are hardly consistent with Holmes's vision. See, e.g., M. T. VanHecke, "Changing Emphases in Specific Performance," 40 *N. Car. L. Rev.* 1 (1961); Alan Schwartz, "The Case for Specific Performance," 89 *Yale L. J.* 271 (1979) (arguing that specific performance should be as routinely available as the damages remedy). But cf. Charles Goetz and Robert Scott, "Liquidated Damages, Penalties and the Just Compensation Principle: Some Notes on an Enforcement Model and a Theory of Efficient Breach," 77 *Colum. L. Rev.* 554, 558-559 (1977). Cf. Snepp v. United States, 444 U.S. 507 (1980) (per curiam), where a former agent of the C.I.A. had breached an employment agreement to provide the agency with a prepublication copy of any writing about agency activities. Finding a fiduciary relationship between the parties, the court affirmed the imposition of a constructive trust on the profits from a book published in violation of the agreement.

8. 115 U.S. 188 (1885).

9. 115 U.S. 213 (1885).

10. See Jacob & Young v. Kent, 230 N.Y. 239, 129 N.E. 889 (1921); Haymore v. Levinson, 8 Utah 2d 66, 328 P.2d 307 (1958).

11. See Inman v. Clyde Hall Drilling Co., 369 P.2d 498 (Alaska 1962).

12. See Unnerzagt v. Prestera, 339 Pa. 141, 13 A.2d 46 (1940). But see Southern Surety Co. v. MacMillan Co., 58 F.2d 541 (10th Cir. 1932).

13. See, e.g., Cities Service Oil Co. v. National Shawmut Bank of Boston, 342 Mass. 108, 172 N.E.2d 104 (1961) (exercise of the option held ineffective when mailed on the last day but received after expiration); The Austin Friars, 71 L.T.R. (n.s.) 27 (Adm. 1894).

14. 193 N.Y. 349, 86 N.E. 1 (1908).

15. Cf. Hand, J., in Mitshubishi Goshi Kaisha v. J. Aron and Co., 16 F.2d 185, 186 (2d Cir. 1926): "There is no room in commercial contracts for the doctrine of substantial performance."

16. See the discussion in chapter 6 supra at 86-89.

17. For a full review of the law of penalties and forfeitures, see Goetz and Scott, supra note 7.

18. This example is based on Jacobs and Young v. Kent, supra note 10.

19. See, e.g., UCC §2-607(2), which provides that acceptance of a nonconforming tender does not of itself impair any other remedy for nonconformity, although under UCC §2-607(3) the buyer must notify the seller of the breach within a reasonable time to preserve his right to damages. See also "Waiver Distributed," in Lon Fuller and Melvin Eisenberg, *Basic Contract Law* 240 (3rd ed. St. Paul, 1972).

20. See Oliver v. Campbell, 43 Cal.2d 298, 273 P.2d 15 (1954). See also Dawson, supra note 2; Farnsworth, supra note 2; Walsh, supra note 3; George Palmer, "The Contract Price as a Limit on Restitution for Defendant's Breach," 20 *Ohio St. L. J.* 264, 266 (1959).

21. See, e.g., Nevins v. Ward, 320 Mass. 70, 67 N.E.2d 673 (1946).

22. See Britton v. Turner, 6 N.H. 281, 26 Am. Dec. 713 (1834) (employee in breach entitled to reasonable value of services rendered). See also Freed-

man v. The Rector, 37 Cal.2d 16, 230 P.2d 629 (1951); Palmer, supra note 20; *Restatement* (1st) §357; *Restatement* (2d) §374.

23. See, e.g., Plotnick v. Pennsylvania Smelting and Refining Co., 194 F.2d 859 (3d Cir. 1952).

24. See, e.g., Koppelon v. Ritter Flooring Corporation, 97 N.J.L. 200, 116 A. 491 (1922). See also Caporale v. Rubine, 92 N.J.L. 463, 105 A. 226 (1918); Hathaway v. Sabin, 63 Vt. 527, 22 A. 633 (1891).

In cases where one party has reasonable grounds for insecurity with respect to the other party's performance, UCC§2-609 gives the insecure party the right to suspend his own performance and to require adequate assurance that the other party will duly perform. If such assurances are not forthcoming within a reasonable time, the aggrieved party may treat the contract as breached by repudiation. See, e.g., Corn Products Refining Co. v. Fasola, 94 N.J.L. 181, 109 A. 505 (1920).

25. This case is based on Hochster v. De la Tour, 118 Eng.Rep. 922 (Q.B. 1853).

26. See "Note, A Suggested Revision of the Contract Doctrine of Anticipatory Repudiation," 64 *Yale L. J.* 85 (1954). See also Calamari and Perillo, supra note 3, at ch. 12, esp. the list of leading articles cited at 456 n. 6.

27. See *Restatement* (2d) §§250, 255.

28. The doctrines of mitigation and anticipatory breach intersect curiously when the anticipatory repudiation is of a contract to deliver in the future goods for which fully functioning futures and spot markets exist. In that case it has generally been held that the injured party is not obliged to mitigate damages by making a second contract for forward delivery, and certainly he need not buy in the spot market. See Reliance Cooperage Corp. v. Treat, 195 F.2d 977 (8th Cir. 1952). Contra, Oloffson v. Coomer, 11 Ill.App.3d 918, 296 N.E.2d 871 (1973). See also 5 Corbin §1053; Note, supra note 26, at 103-105; Anthony Kronman and Richard Posner, *The Economics of Contract Law* 160-161 (Boston, 1979).

29. See Immanuel Kant, *Groundwork of the Metaphysics of Morals* 41 (Paton ed. trans., Harper Torchbooks ed. New York, 1964); Mary Gregor, *Laws of Freedom* xii-xiii (Oxford, 1963).

# INDEX

*Leitch Gold Mines, Ltd. v. Texas Gulf
  Sulphur,* 148
Lewis, D., 15
Liberalism: caricature of, 149; concep-
  tion of contract, 3, 11, 140, 143,
  144, 149; political theory, 71-73,
  94-95, 104-107, 110
Liberty, *see* Autonomy
*Lingenfelder v. Wainwright Brewery
  Co.,* 141
*Linz v. Shuck,* 141
Llewellyn, K., 40, 136, 143, 144, 150
Locke, D., 137, 138
Loyalty, 85, 88, 120-121
Lying, 9-11, 37n, 78-79, 100
Lyons, D., 138

MacCormick, N., 137
Macneil, I., 3, 76, 77, 84
Macpherson, C. B., 136
McNeilly, F. S., 137
Mack, E., 153
Mailbox rule, 50-52
Maine, H. S., 76
Malice, 55, 89n, 97, 100, 102,
  103n
Market, 5, 36-37, 71-72, 94, 104-108
*Marks Realty Co. v. Hotel Hermitage
  Co.,* 146
Marriage, *see* Family relations
Marx, K., 151
Meaning, 60, 64, 87, 89. *See also*
  Language
Melville, H., 152
Mercy, 20
*M. F. Kemper Construction Co. v.
  City of Los Angeles,* 145, 148
Michelman, F. I., 152
*Mills v. Wyman,* 33, 141
Mistakes, 20, 25, 57-73, 81-82, 105n;
  mutual, 63; unilateral, 61-63, 81-82
Mitigation, 131
*Mitshubishi Goshi Kaisha v. J. Aron
  and Co.,* 155
Model Penal Code, 151
Modifications, 28, 33-35
*Monge v. Beeke Rubber Co.,* 89n
Monopoly, 107
Moral consideration, 31-33
Morality: and contract law, 1, 2, 7,
  8, 14-17, 68, 78, 97, 98, 112,
  131-132
Motive, 30, 130, 143. *See also*
  Malice
Murray, J., 150
Musgrave, P., 153
Musgrave, R., 153

Mutuality of obligation, 29, 31, 86
  117

*Nagel, In re,* 131
Neofotistos v. Harvard Brewing Co.,
  86, 89
*Nevins v. Ward,* 155
*Newman and Snell's State Bank v.
  Hunter,* 31-32
New York Workman's Comp. Law, 152
Non-liquet, 67
Nordstrom, R., 154
*Norrington v. Wright,* 118-120
Notice of breach, 131n
Nozick, R., 95, 135, 142, 154

*Obde v. Schlemeyer,* 78-82
Objective standard, 60-78
Obligation, 14-17. *See also*
  Morality
Offers, 45-48, 95-96; withdrawal of,
  54-56; crossed, 53-54
*Oliver v. Campbell,* 155
*Oloffson v. Coomer,* 156
Options, 31, 36, 39, 48, 116-117

Page, W., 143
Palmer, G., 125n, 154, 155
*Paradine v. Jane,* 146
Paternalism, 20, 105n
Patterson, E., 141-142, 144, 145,
  150
*Patterson v. Meyerhofer,* 85, 86
Peetz, V., 43
Perdue, W., 4, 138, 147, 154
Perillo, J., 154
Perkins, R., 151
Pigou, A., 148
*Plotnick v. Pennsylvania Smelting and
  Refining Co.,* 156
Positivism, legal, 67
Posner, R., 5, 9, 144, 151, 153, 156
*Post v. Jones,* 109-111
Pothier, R.-J., 139
Pound, R., 136, 140, 142, 147, 151
Poverty, 105-106, 153
Powell, R., 151
Prichard, H., 137, 138
Private sphere, 135
Privity of contract, 23
Promissory estoppel, 25n
Property, 37, 82, 99-103; transferabil-
  ity of, 37
Prosser, W., 139, 148, 149
Pufendorf, S. von, 21, 142

Radin, M., 136

INDEX